3 1312 00098 555

D0695914

BE

YOUR

OWN

DETECTIVE

BE
YOUR
OWN
DETECTIVE

Greg Fallis and Ruth Greenberg

M. EVANS AND COMPANY   NEW YORK

Library of Congress Cataloging-in-Publication Data

Fallis, Greg.
  Be your own detective / Greg Fallis and Ruth Greenberg.
    p. cm.
  Includes bibliographical references.
  ISBN 0-87131-579-3
  1. Private investigators. I. Greenberg, Ruth. II. Title.
HV8085.F28 1989   89-23676
363.2′89′02373—dc20

M. Evans and Company, Inc.
216 East 49 Street
New York, New York 10017

Design by Cynthia Dunne

Manufactured in the United States of America

9 8 7 6 5 4 3 2 1

To these investigators, who gave me so much without always knowing it. This book I give to you.

Frank H., good as family, a quick and liberal hand at the bottle, and always game for outlandish enterprise. I have no higher praise.

Anita G., the only northern light I saw on those surreal road shows to the wilds of Maine.

Bruce S., who kept me out of almost as much trouble as he got me into.

And especially Betsy K., for reasons too numerous to catalog.

G.F.

And to Thurgood Marshall, Ted Kennedy, Joe Biden, David Garfunkel, and my mom and dad. They know why.

R.G.

Contents

ACKNOWLEDGMENT

The authors would like to express their sincere appreciation to Susannah, without whom this enterprise would not have been possible.

INTRODUCTION

I'm a criminal lawyer. I know what detectives do. And I know you can learn to do it, too.

Almost a thousand people accused of crimes have come to me for help. Some were innocent. Most were guilty.

The innocent needed me to find out what really happened. The guilty wanted me to get them off the hook. For both these jobs, I needed a detective.

For a long time, Greg Fallis was the man for the job. I found the law, he found the facts. I knew the library and the courtroom, he knew the courtroom and the world. We were a team. Sometimes we won.

Sometimes, after court was over for the day, we'd sit around drinking and talking. And Greg would tell stories about his job, some of the same stories he tells here. It was a world far different from the courtroom. I wanted to know it. I thought it would make me a better lawyer. I asked him to teach me and he agreed.

At first I went with him on the job. I did what he said. I learned a lot. I got the basic tools.

And it was tough going, those nights in smoke-filled

bars, those days in line at the Department of Motor Vehicles. Sometimes I had to wear a down jacket, sometimes a suit, stockings, and pearls. I looked at blood, at broken boards, and at thousands of dull documents. I smelled burned buildings and leftover fried chicken. I talked to many men, women, children, and dogs, and I learned a trade very different from my own.

So can you.

To guide you, I've added some stories from my own experience along the way. And to guard you from legal peril, I've included a chapter on the detective and the law.

Before you begin, two very important warnings from these years as a criminal lawyer.

1. Sometimes you'll never know what really happened.

In police shows there's almost always a solution. In real life, most police like to think there's a solution. That way someone goes to jail, and we all feel safe.

But the true detective knows sometimes you can't know. There is a limit to this art. Know your limit.

2. Sometimes you'll find out what really happened.

Let's imagine a forty-year-old alcoholic burglar, female, who has a fourteen-year-old retarded child confined to a wheelchair. The burglar moves in with a fellow who is fond of children. So fond, that one night he makes love to the crippled girl, who bears a child. The fellow goes to jail for statutory rape, and the baby is given to a nice family who loves her. Do you want to tell her who her birth parents are?

Remember what happened when Eve picked the apple, and when Pandora opened the box. Not all knowledge is good.

A talk show host, hearing about this book, asked us, "Aren't you worried that when you teach people how to do these things, they'll get themselves into trouble? Maybe commit crimes? Aren't you afraid of what people will do with the information?"

The simple answer is no. I'm sworn to uphold the Constitution and the Constitution upholds our right to speak freely. I don't think a person can have too much information.

This book provides access to skills and techniques that you can use for good or for evil. You can operate within or outside the law. As a member in good standing of the bar, I advise you to obey the law. As to good or evil, because I am a member of the bar, I don't advise.

You can learn to be your own detective. You can eat the apple, you can open the box. But be careful. Once you know, you can't forget.

R.G.

FOREWORD

'm going to tell you how to do the things detectives do. Real detectives, not the ones you see on television or read about in novels. Real-life detective work can't be started and completed in sixty minutes. Nor can it be arranged around commercial breaks. It's tough, lonely work; it's difficult to do well and frequently unappreciated.

But if you want to know how to do it, I'll teach you. I'll tell you how to find people, how to watch them and follow them, how to get them to talk to you and tell you the things you want to know. I'll tell you how to develop information sources and how to work your way through a maze of official files.

I'll teach you what I've learned, the techniques I've acquired through experience and from other detectives. I'll give you examples of how those techniques are used. I'll tell you what has worked for me. I'll also tell you the things that haven't worked.

I'll let you into the world of the detective by the back door.

But as you read this book and examine the techniques, try to think of other ways to achieve the same results. Don't accept what you read as gospel; what you read here are merely suggestions based on what has worked for me and for others in the same profession. Ask yourself how the techniques could be adapted to suit your own personality. There are very few rules in detective work, but there is one overriding precept—question everything.

After all, that's what being a detective is all about.

When I first began work as a detective, I was overwhelmed. There was so much I didn't know. My first assignment involved finding witnesses to a hit-and-run accident that had taken place on a sparsely populated road. It was a simple assignment on the face of it. A few weeks earlier a car had jammed on its brakes causing a motorcycle to smash into it from behind. The motorcycle was demolished and the rider thrown onto the trunk of the car. When the driver of the car sped off, the motorcyclist rolled off the trunk into a ditch.

All I had to do was find somebody who had seen it happen.

My first task was to go to the scene. When I got there, my excitement dimmed. There were only a few houses within half a mile of the accident site. Not a lot of potential witnesses. Hoping for the best, I went to the closest house and knocked on the door. Nobody answered. But the television was playing loudly and I knew somebody was in the house. I knocked louder, with the same result.

Already I was stumped. Should I go to the back door? The back door was behind a chain-link fence, but the gate was open. Would that be trespassing?

Should I peek in at the windows? Was that legal? Maybe I should just leave and come back later. Maybe the person in the house had had an accident and was unable to come to the door. Maybe he, or she, was unconscious. Maybe dead. Maybe murdered by the hit-and-run driver. I pounded on the door wildly, and, of course, a very pleasant—and very deaf—old woman eventually answered the door. No, she hadn't seen anything on the night in question. Plainly, she hadn't *heard* anything.

It was the same at the other houses. None of the others were actually hearing impaired, but they might as well have been stone deaf, and blind as the sailor Pew. Nobody had seen or heard a thing.

Now I was really stumped. I couldn't think of anything else to do. I felt like a failure. So I called another detective. "Did you put an ad in the paper asking for witnesses?" she asked. "Have you checked body shops to see if anybody had any repairs consistent with the accident? Have you gone to the scene at the same time as the accident and written down the license numbers of cars driving by?" And, of course, I hadn't. "Then get off your butt and get out there," she said.

And I did. I went out there and found three witnesses. All I needed was somebody to give me a few ideas.

That's what I'm going to do for you. I'll teach you the basic techniques; I'll give you a few ideas. But in order for them to work, you'll have to get yourself out there. As I said before, that's what the job is all about.

BE

YOUR

OWN

DETECTIVE

The incidents and cases presented in this book are based on actual events. To protect the clients involved, however, some of the facts and circumstances have been altered or fictionalized. Some examples are composites of more than one case.

Chapter 1

WHAT IT TAKES

Greg arrives in town, one he's never been in before. He never expected to be there, so he has no map. It's getting dark. He doesn't know anybody, doesn't know where he is or where he's going. But he's got to find a man who works in a bar near the railroad.

And, as if guided by an invisible hand, he drives directly to the bar and is soon drinking a long-neck Bud and talking to that man.

Greg never asks for directions. But he always seems to know where to find a decent meal, or a gas station, or a killer bar.

How does he do it? How was he able to find Eulonia, Georgia, without a map? I finally asked him how.

"Luck," he said. "I have good luck."

It takes luck to be a good detective. And it takes practice, because in this business you make your own luck.

All things being equal, I hire the experienced detective. All towns are not alike, but after you've seen a hundred new towns you know where the train tracks *are and where a bar will be. And after a thousand new towns, you forget you ever had to learn it and you call yourself lucky. Just lucky.*

When I have a child, I'll teach her to be a detective. I'll take her for long rides in the car and ask her, "Can you show Mommy and Daddy how to get home?" I'll take her for a walk and say, "Tell me what you saw." I'll teach her to pay attention from a very early age. That's what Greg's parents did.

I understand that tiny gumshoes can be bronzed.

R.G.

What does it take to be a good detective? Novels and movies would have you believe all it takes is broad shoulders and a thick skull. Or a mind like a computer. Or just a trench coat and a gun.

Real life, as always, is more mundane, and more complex.

What it really takes to be a detective—a good detective—is a peculiar blend of talents and attitudes. This quality isn't unique to detectives. The same could be said of the practitioners of almost any field—surgeons, mechanics, architects. Even mass murderers. If you have the potential, you can learn the necessary skills.

In detective work *what* you are is often less important than *who* you are. In may ways gender, race, physical ability, and such are irrelevant. Those factors can be either a liability or an asset. It all depends on the circumstance and the person.

Let me deal with the gender issue right away.

Throughout this book I'll refer to the detective as *he*. I don't do this because men are better detectives. I do it because it's practical and the only gender-neutral pronoun we have is *it*.

I know a detective who specializes in defending people accused of murder, people charged with the most savage and vicious acts imaginable. Murder is serious business; only the best detectives are called upon to work on such cases. This detective is about five foot two, weighs maybe a hundred pounds, and is the mother of two pretty daughters.

I'll repeat myself. *Who* you are—the kind of person you are—is more important than *what* you are. You can have shoulders like Superman and a brain like Albert Einstein, but if you don't know what to do with them, you might as well stay in bed.

I'm going to tell you what it takes; in later chapters I'll tell you what to do with it. Whether you put those skills to use is up to you.

I've divided the qualities of a good detective among four categories:

1. The intellectual

2. The social

3. The emotional

4. The physical

These categories are interrelated. They overlap one another, which is how it should be. The detective craft is built on gray areas.

The Intellectual Qualities

You needn't be Sherlock Holmes to be a good detective. While intelligence is important, this isn't rocket science and a stratospheric IQ isn't a prerequisite. Still, the craft does make certain intellectual demands. A good detective needs—

- Street sense
- Analytic ability
- Curiosity
- Tangential knowledge

You already have each of these qualities to some extent, probably to a greater degree than you realize. You need only become more aware of them to be able to put them to use.

Street Sense

Street sense is an intuitive understanding of the way the world works and how people move through it. It's a feeling you develop. Like a lot of intuitive processes, street sense can be developed and, once developed, refined. The more time you spend on the streets and the more attention you pay to detail, the sharper your street sense will become.

Once I was training a new investigator, helping him find a witness to a drug-related assault. We'd learned that the witness often slept in the hallway of a certain seedy tenement. As we entered a back stairwell of the building, we interrupted four men involved in a drug sale. Although no drugs, weapons, or money were in plain view, it was clear what was taking place. At least it was clear to me. The new investigator had no idea what we'd walked into. He knew something was wrong, he felt the tension. And he stopped dead still. It was the worst thing he could have done.

Had we just nodded and continued up the stairs, we would almost certainly have been ignored. But by stopping, he had thrown sand in the system. A drug sale is a volatile situation. Each party involved has to control his suspicion of the other long enough to make the exchange. Neither side wants to see strangers blundering onto the scene. Strangers mean trouble. Everybody has to assume a stranger works for the other side. It's just good business.

We all stood very still for a long moment. Then I patted my pockets, turned to the other investigator, and said I thought I'd dropped my car keys outside. I suggested we go look for them. I hadn't lost my keys, of course. I just wanted an excuse to get the hell out of there.

The new investigator's street sense was developed enough to know there was danger, but not enough to know why. When he asked how I knew, I found it difficult to answer. There was something about their posture, about the degree of intensity in the way they watched each other, about the aggressive caution in their eyes when we barged in. I just knew.

The only way you can sharpen your street sense is to spend time there. This doesn't mean you need to hang out with drug dealers. It just means you need to go out there and look. Take walks and pay attention to the people you see. What are they doing? How do they carry themselves? What information can you discern from what you see?

Go to a bar, even if you don't drink. Order a beer and quietly look around. Notice how the people interact. Can you identify the regulars? How?

Pay attention. I'll repeat these words frequently. Pay attention to everything. You can sort out what matters later.

Analytic Ability

A detective uses his analytical powers to solve problems. He takes seemingly unconnected bits of information and fits them together to form a plausible and logical account of the events. It takes an agile mind, one capable of looking at a set of facts from many different perspectives, and willing to view those facts objectively.

A good detective sees connections other people wouldn't. The connections are always there; nothing exists in a vacuum. Your job is to find them.

Curiosity

As we all know, curiosity killed the cat. But a cat wouldn't be a cat without it, neither would a detective be a detective. Every good detective I know is intensely curious. It's not always an appealing quality, and, if not kept under control, it can get you or your client into trouble. There are questions that need not be asked, answers that need not be sought.

I had a client who was charged with a major felony, a crime he claimed he hadn't committed. The client said he was on Cape Cod the weekend of the crime, but he couldn't recall the name of the motel he had stayed in.

I was skeptical—alibis so rarely pan out. But not so skeptical that I was willing to pass up a chance to spend some time on the Cape. So I went to the village the client had claimed he'd visited, nosed around, and, to my surprise, found the motel. I even talked the manager into giving me a copy of the registration ticket.

The only problem was the time he had checked in. It was just barely possible that he could have committed the crime and still had time to drive to Cape Cod by the time shown on the motel registration. He would have had to drive like a madman and violate every speed law in existence, but everybody drives that way in Massachusetts.

I probably didn't need to do anything more. The registration most likely would have been sufficient to establish reasonable doubt before a jury. But I was curious. I still had questions. I had to see if I could find witnesses to place the client in that village *before* he checked in to the motel, to establish beyond any doubt that he couldn't have committed the crime.

And I did.

In a bar near the motel I found three people who could swear the client was at that bar before checking in to the motel; three people who could clear him. But we couldn't use them as witnesses. Why? Because the client was in the bar selling those witnesses drugs.

Sometimes you can better serve your client (or yourself) by not asking questions, by not looking for all the answers. It seems sort of unnatural, like trying to teach a cat not to hunt, but at times it must be so.

That knowledge of the client's criminal activity precluded me from being a witness as well. If I testified, all the prosecutor had to do was ask, "During your investigation, Mr. Fallis, did you come across any information that your client had committed a crime?" The defense attorney would object, of course, and I wouldn't have to answer the question. But the jury would know we were hiding something.

Tangential Knowledge

Tangential knowledge is what you call those odd bits of information you collect over the years, information with seemingly little practical use. Baseball statistics, for example, or a knowledge of plate tectonics, or an understanding of the nesting habits of wrens. Other than game-show contestants and writers, detectives are probably the only people in the world who find use for such information.

Why does a detective need a large fund of tangential information? Because you never know what sort of information might be important.

I needed to interview a doctor, a trauma specialist, who'd examined the victim of an assault. I met him during a quiet period at the emergency room. But he didn't want to speak with me. He was busy reading a book.

A book. One man had been badly injured and another was facing a long prison term and this guy was too busy to talk to me because he was reading *a book*. Then I saw the title of the book; it was the play *Juno and the Paycock*, by Sean O'Casey. The doctor was an amateur thespian.

So instead of asking him about the case, I talked to him about the play. I don't know much about theater, but I do know a little about Irish history (the play takes place during the Anglo-Irish War). For the next half-hour we discussed Ireland and the Irish. Then he told me everything I wanted to know about the case.

There's no way I could have known how to prepare for that interview. I was just lucky I knew something the doctor was interested in. It doesn't always work so well. There have been a lot of interviews I might have gotten if I'd known anything about auto mechanics.

You know similar sorts of things. Maybe not about the history of Ireland, but things. How to tile a bathroom, where to find good, fresh produce, how a barometer works.

Build on that knowledge. Read a lot. It doesn't matter what, just read. Anything. Science fiction, gothic novels, ingredient labels, any words in a row. And listen to other people, even if they're dull. They know stuff, too, and are willing to share it with you. In fact, dull people *insist* on sharing it. Read, listen, and pay attention.

Most of what you learn will never be useful. It's extremely unlikely you'll ever need to be able to discuss coracles, or the feeding habits of small-mouth bass, or the rules of bocce ball.

But you might.

The Social Qualities

When I say a good detective needs good social skills I don't mean he needs to be able to tell a soupspoon from a salad fork. Although that never hurts. What I mean is that the abilities to communicate effectively, to establish quick rapport, and to appear comfortable in almost any situation are critical skills.

A good detective needs—

1. Good listening skills

2. The ability to put others at ease

3. Good acting skills

4. The ability to speak at the level of your audience

5. An understanding of body language

Trying to do business without these skills is like trying to eat your soup with a salad fork.

A really good detective can fit in to almost any social situation, even an unfamiliar one. How? By staying calm, acting as if you belong, and paying attention.

I know an investigator who tailed a subject to a Catholic church one Sunday morning. It was a big church with a lot of exits, and the investigator was afraid his subject would be able to slip out a side door when the mass was over. He also wanted to know if the subject was meeting somebody in the church.

So he followed the man in. Not such a big deal, except the investigator is Jewish. Once inside he was suddenly surrounded by a totally alien culture. He didn't know when to stand up, when to sit down, when to kneel. He didn't know the hymns or the responses to the litany, didn't even know what a litany was. He was familiar with the concept of communion, but had no idea what a communion wafer looked like, how it was taken, or if taking communion could be avoided without drawing attention to himself. He was absolutely lost.

But he stayed calm, smiled politely, and paid attention to the people around him. He stood up when they did, knelt when they did. He lip-synced the words to the hymns. He noticed that a few people (including the man he was tailing) did not go forward to receive communion, so stayed seated also.

Ernest Hemingway defined courage as grace under pressure. I don't know much about courage—it seems too fine a word to be used in detective work. But I can't think of a better description for the way that investigator handled that situation—grace under pressure.

Having good social skills doesn't preclude you from being rude; they just allow you to choose the occasion. There is nothing to gain by being rude out of ignorance.

I'll cover these topics in more detail in the chapter on verbal seduction.

The Emotional Qualities

The emotional demands of the detective's craft can be divided into two categories—those that are functions of the job and those that are its result. The former are occupational demands; the latter are personal. Either kind can be severe.

Occupational Demands

Detective work is odd. Just about every important decision you make is based on information you know to be incomplete. And those decisions have to be made with the knowledge that your course of action is limited. Such odd work requires an equally odd assortment of emotional qualities. In order to remain effective, a detective needs—

- Professional distance
- Persistence
- A high tolerance for stress
- A strong sense of self

Professional Distance I learned about professional distance as a medic in the service. I was only nineteen and suddenly in a position in which I had to make life-and-death decisions. The only way I could do the job well was to detach myself emotionally from what was going on. Even when in a crisis I pretended to be calm and in control. And people believed it. Then a strange thing would happen; the other people would calm down. And then an even stranger thing happened; I myself became calm and in control.

The same lesson applies to detectives, or anybody else. You cannot be effective when you're scared, or disgusted, or angry, or even elated. Any powerful emotion weakens your objectivity and clouds your judgment.

Persistence It's easy to give up. There are

times when the desire to throw up your hands in despair is almost irresistible.

I was trying to find a witness in a felony case. The witness, however, did not want to be found. He abandoned his apartment and quit his job. I spoke to his neighbors, his former co-workers, his friends, his landlord. Nobody seemed to know where he was. But on his rental agreement and his employment application the man had listed his grandmother as his next of kin.

So I locked on to the grandmother. I staked out her house, hoping he'd show up. I tailed her everywhere she went. I went through her trash for her old telephone bills and called all the numbers. I got the description of his car from the Department of Motor Vehicles in case he drove by her house.

And it paid off. It took a while, but one Sunday afternoon he showed up at his grandmother's house. I waited until he finished his visit, then took him.

As I said, it's easy to give up. Surrender is tempting. When you're facing a brick wall, you have three choices. You can give up and walk away (a reasonable response). You can try to sneak around or over it (my favorite). Or you can just pound your head against it until you break through.

On the other hand, you need to know when persistence slips over the line into obstinacy. You should persist as long as there is a reasonable chance of success (and then just a little longer). Then give it up.

High Tolerance for Stress One of the vexations of detective work is that you alternate between periods of boredom and moments of near panic. You're often involved in situations where you don't fully understand what's happening and have little control over the events taking place. You have to make vitally important decisions based on woefully inadequate information. This is stressful, to say the least.

Stress, frustration, ambiguity, and boredom. These are the detective's version of the four horsemen of the Apocalypse. If you can't deal with them, go work in a hardware store.

Each detective handles stress differently. Some meditate, some take up hobbies, some drink too much. I can't tell you what is best. I haven't decided for myself yet.

Sense of Self We all want people to like us, to appreciate us, to think well of us. Detectives are no different. But sometimes detectives have to behave in ways that don't represent who they really are.

There are times when you have to look stupid or bumbling. Or accept insults you ordinarily wouldn't. Or allow others to see you in an unflattering light. In order to do that, you need a strong feeling for who you are.

During a strike at a local factory I was asked to interview some replacement workers who had witnessed an assault. One of the strikers had been badly beaten by a pair of strikebreakers. The witnesses agreed to talk to me, but only at the plant. That meant I had to cross the picket line. I'd never crossed a picket line in my life.

I supported the strike. I was working for one of the strikers. I even had friends who worked at the plant and were on the picket line. But I couldn't stop to explain why I was crossing the line. It would have

alienated the people I was going to interview if I was
spotted visiting with the strikers.

As I drove through the gate of the plant, the strikers shouted at me and called me a scab. They spit on
my car. I felt like the lowest of the low. I knew I was
doing the right thing, but there was little comfort in
the knowledge.

A good detective has to appreciate and respect
himself. And can't depend on anybody else to.

Personal Demands

Dashiell Hammett wrote a short story in which he
describes an aging detective: "... his gentle eyes
behind gold spectacles and his mild smile, hiding the
fact that fifty years of sleuthing had left him without
any feelings at all on any subject."

Hammett had been a detective. He understood that
the greatest risk faced by the detective is that of
becoming emotionally sterile. It isn't the danger of
getting beat up or shot, it's the danger of losing emotional balance. Detectives are forced (or allowed) to
look at the dark sides of human nature. They often
see an intensity of emotion that forces them to
respond by becoming cold and distant. They see
much that is pathetic, corrupt, and ugly. Sometimes
they see too much.

Since the job tends to be solitary, it allows time for
introspection and reflecting on what you've seen.
There is danger of becoming hard and cynical; there
is danger in *not* becoming hard and cynical. And even
more perilous is the possibility for abandonment of
compassion and humanity.

Near my office was a small store where I would stop two or three times a week to buy a soft drink. The store was owned by a cantankerous old woman who kept a couple of cats and an arthritic dog. After a few months she saw I liked her animals and became a little less crabby. Eventually we began to visit, and I learned she was peevish just because she was old and tired.

One winter day I went to the store and found it surrounded by police cruisers. The old woman had been robbed and murdered. She and her dog had been stabbed to death. A few days later I was assigned to help in the defense of a person accused of killing her.

One of my duties was to photograph the scene. As a medic I'd become accustomed to gore, so the dried blood on the floor and the walls wasn't disturbing in itself. And as I immersed myself in the business of shooting the photographs, I forgot who the blood belonged to. In order to shoot one particular spatter pattern, I had to stand in a corner where the blood had pooled. Blood, when it dries, becomes flaky, and it crunched under my sneakers.

I finished the job and began to walk back to my office. For some reason I turned and looked back toward the store. I saw I was leaving a trail of faint, copper-colored footprints behind me. I checked the bottom of my sneakers. Some of the crusted blood had stuck in the grooves.

For a moment I was paralyzed with horror and felt like screaming. But only for a moment. Habit and training took over. I swished my shoes in a puddle of melting snow, calming myself as the blood speckled the puddle. Then I walked back to my office.

It's tough to find a healthy balance between compassion and emotional self-defense. But you must. If you don't, you may wind up an emotional eunuch like Hammett's detective. Or curled up in a ball in your closet, silently screaming.

The Physical Qualities

This is the least important attribute of the detective. You don't need to be strong, you don't need to be nimble, you don't need to be in perfect physical condition. Those things can be helpful, but they're not critical.

Still, you ought to be in reasonably good shape. You won't have to run a marathon, but you may have to tail a fast walker. You won't have to bench press twice your body weight, but you may have to move some heavy boxes.

What *is* critical is stamina. A good detective needs the ability and, more important, the willingness to endure. Not just to persist in the face of long hours, solitude, and stress, but endure actual physical discomfort as well. The aching feet and knees after hours of standing and walking, the back and eye strain from long hours spent hunched over countless ledgers in some poorly lit office, the upset stomach from too many indigestible meals eaten on the run.

Television detectives suffer, and shrug off, bullet wounds and concussions. Real detectives have more mundane afflictions—hemorrhoids, indigestion, and tension headaches.

Not very romantic, is it?

I hope by now you have some idea what it takes to

be a good detective. I also hope you examine yourself carefully, that you give yourself the same cold and objective scrunity you'd give to a case, to see if you have what it takes. Because the last thing the world needs is another bad investigator.

In later chapters I'll suggest investigative techniques you might want to try. There are a lot of reasons *not* to try them. You might make a mistake and look foolish; somebody might get upset with you; you could waste a lot of time.

Those are good reasons. I feel the same way. I doubt I'd do them unless I was getting paid. But you must, you absolutely *must*, be willing to look foolish, to waste time, to risk the anger of others when the circumstance demands it.

That's all it takes. Nothing really out of the ordinary. Just ordinary things in extraordinary combinations. And a willingness to put your client's needs before your own.

You can do it. The question you have to ask is this: Do you really want to?

Chapter 2

THE GENTLE ART
OF TAILING

When we were working in Key West one week Greg taught me how to tail. I recommend the Keys for the beginning detective. Everybody wears dark glasses and brightly colored clothes, and everybody is looking at everybody else.

There are lots of bars in Key West, and all of them seem to have mirrors. Mirrors, as you'll learn, are a detective's dream.

Sadly, I discovered that the caution I take when practicing law, checking and double checking every step, got in my way when I tried to practice tailing. Too much can happen while you're being careful.

I learned how to tail on the flat ground of Florida. About a year later I was trying to tail a guy in San Francisco, where the entire town is built on hills, and the sidewalks have stairs. I discovered three things about tailing in San Francisco: (1) I have a tendency to watch my feet going down stairs, (2) you can't watch your subject and your feet at the same time, and (3) if

you try *to watch your subject and your feet at the*
same time, you fall down.

R.G.

In this chapter you will learn how to perform a solo tail, both on foot and by car. You will learn to blend in with a crowd, to alter your appearance, to identify your subject from a distance. You'll learn the significance of details, and how to use shield cars. This is the true stuff.

Tailing is the quintessence of the detective's craft, the distillate of all the detective's skills blended into a strange, complex, and heady drink. It's often frustrating, sometimes tiring, and occasionally frightening. But when it works, it is intoxicating.

Tailing requires a feel for the behavior of the individual and the crowd. You have to be in tune with the person you're tailing and with the people around you. You have to balance risk and caution, confidence and cockiness, anxiety and need. You must be patient; you must be alert; you must be intuitive and clever and persistent. Above all, you must be invisible. You must be like a mist in comfortable shoes.

As with most detective work, there are no solid rules to tailing. Well, there is one—don't get caught.

Being spotted by your subject (detectives usually say getting "made" or "burned") is more than a failure of technique, it can be fatal to the investigation.

Tailing is a reactive skill. Your subject acts—you react. You can try to anticipate his behavior, even predict it. But it's an egregious mistake to rely on that prediction. If you feel the need to prove how clever you are (and most of us do occasionally), make mental bets with yourself about what your subject will do. But never put the job at risk.

Generally, tailing is done in one of two ways—

- On foot
- By car

Though these are the most common ways, you're not restricted to them. People have been followed by aircraft and boat (a remarkable number of philanderers want to make love on the high seas). Detectives have used bicycles, golf carts, you name it. I know a detective who tailed his subject jogging in the park. Anywhere people go, there is a detective willing to follow.

Ideally, a tail is performed by a team of operatives in frequent communication by radio. Usually, though, such a production is prohibitively expensive and most often the detective must conduct a solo tail.

Even working solo, you begin with a singular advantage: Very few people expect to be followed. That only happens in the movies. Even so, some people are more suspicious than others. Women having affairs tend to be more cautious than men, but even errant wives find it difficult to believe that another person would actually follow them everywhere they go.

Offsetting this advantage is a random universe. People and events are unpredictable, and the detective is at the mercy of all their whims and vagaries. Seemingly rational people will come to a tire-screeching halt at a yard sale, leaving you to go sailing by, desperately looking for an inconspicuous place to pull over. Or you'll stub your toe on an uneven sidewalk and your subject will disappear while you hop up and down on one foot and mutter useless curses. On one occasion I lost a subject when I was stopped by a police officer and lectured for jaywalking. It was probably the only time in the history of that city that a person was actually stopped for jaywalking.

On Foot

This is the way most people picture a detective—shadowing some shady character down into the city's bowels. They conjure up an image of a lone man in a trench coat leaning against a street lamp, pretending to read a newspaper.

It's not like that. You can dress like Sam Spade if you want, and lean against any number of lamp poles, and enjoy your image of yourself. Or you can do the job. Conducting a solo tail on foot is a difficult and sensitive task. But with a little preparation, patience, and practice, it's one you can do.

Preparation

The key to conducting a solo tail is preparation. The motto, "Be prepared," is one thing, probably the only thing, detectives have in common with Boy Scouts.

Study your subject. If possible, interview someone who knows him—or her—well. Try to examine recent photographs. Look for gross features that are unlikely to change, such as—

- the shape of the head
- the slope of the shoulders
- the length of the legs

Disregard such small features as eye color or ear shape; if you're close enough to your subject to determine his eye color, you're too close. Besides, the subject is rarely facing you. That's why they call it tailing.

There are a lot of details to note during the initial phases of the tail. For example:

- The subject's walk
- The subject's posture
- The subject's clothing
- Idiosyncratic gestures

Almost everybody has a distinctive walk, a bounce in the step or a tendency to drag his heels. You'll find most people grow into their walk—the younger the subject, the less distinctive the walk.

Posture can be equally characteristic. Many people can be easily identified by the way they carry themselves. A good slouch or hypercorrect posture is a gift to a detective. I once tailed a retired Marine Corps sergeant. I could have followed him in the dark just by listening for the sharp heel strikes of his military stride.

Pay attention to the subject's clothing, but don't use it as your primary means of identification. Clothing, although often distinct, is unreliable. If a person suspects he is being followed, his clothing is the first thing he'll switch. But even people who go to the effort of changing their clothes usually neglect to put on different shoes, and almost never switch their wristwatch.

Finally, note the subject's idiosyncratic gestures. Does he have a nervous habit of straightening his tie? Or perhaps a woman with long hair frequently brushes it out of her face, or just gives a distinctive flick of her head. Pay attention.

Becoming familiar with such distinguishing characteristics is not as difficult as it sounds. You can probably identify your friends and family from a distance that renders their facial features a blur. Baseball fans can often tell players apart by the way they swing the bat. All it requires is that you exercise your powers of observation.

Tactics

Unless you are using electronic location devices, you have to keep your subject in sight. This doesn't mean you need to keep in constant direct visual contact with your subject; in fact, staring at the subject will likely draw his attention. Most detectives are slightly superstitious. Some primitive instinct makes us think a subject can "feel" us if we watch too closely.

So a good detective rarely looks directly at the subject being followed, choosing instead to rely on such aids as—

- Reflections
- Peripheral vision
- "Placing" the subject

The city is full of reflective surfaces—car and shop windows, for example, or those plexiglass bus shelters, even puddles. Use them. Reflections are the detective's friends.

When there are no reflective surfaces, use your peripheral vision. You can determine the width of your peripheral vision by holding your arms directly out in front of you with a pencil in each hand. Look straight ahead at a fixed spot and slowly move your arms apart until you can no longer see the pencils. You can (and should) practice using your peripheral vision. A simple exercise you can do at any time is, again stare straight ahead at a fixed point and note the objects you can see out of the corner of your eye. People process a lot more visual information than they realize. Our brains selectively eliminate most of the information they receive because it's irrelevant. With just a little practice, you can literally widen your horizons.

Visually "placing" your subject is a critical tailing technique. *Placing* simply means noting the subject's direction in relation to yours and estimating his speed of travel and the direction in which he is moving. It allows you to maintain contact with the subject without having to focus all your attention on him. That way you can avoid tripping on the sidewalk or colliding with other pedestrians.

The two most critical elements in maintaining contact are (1) distance and (2) direction.

Proper tailing distance depends entirely on the situation. You need to be close enough to identify the subject and to be able to react to unexpected moves on his part. But you should remain far enough away that you don't attract his attention. In a crowd you can (in fact, you must) follow a little more closely. On nearly deserted streets, allow the subject more distance, even at the risk of losing him. It's better to break off the tail than to get "made" and alert the subject. Good detectives know when to invoke the O'Hara Rule: Tomorrow is another day.

Direction, in this instance, means where the subject is in relation to where you are. A solo tail is almost always conducted from behind the subject. But this doesn't mean you're locked on to the same side of the street. Tailing a subject from the opposite side of the street decreases the risk of being spotted. But, as you might guess, every advantage carries its risk. Your line of sight can be blocked by traffic or parked vehicles; the use of reflective surfaces becomes riskier; crossing the street in a hurry can attract attention, and put you in danger from traffic.

I know a detective who, on a long-term solo tail, followed his subject from the front. He bought a cyclist's mirror (an inexpensive mirror the size of a quarter designed to be attached to cycling helmets and caps with an alligator clip) and attached it to the visor of his baseball cap. Although the limited viewing surface of the mirror made it tricky, he was able to keep an eye on the subject behind him. I wouldn't recommend this as a standard technique, but it could be useful under the proper circumstances.

Clothing

A long-term tail always increases the odds of getting made. To reduce those odds, the detective needs to be as nondescript as possible. This fact is often overlooked by Hollywood. The television detective's carefully styled hair and flashy clothes would condemn a real detective, even assuming he could afford the wardrobe.

Again, there are no firm rules, but here are a few general guidelines:

1. Avoid bright colors. They attract attention.

2. Wear comfortable shoes. This is critical. Assume you'll be on your feet for a long time. I prefer sneakers over any other kind.

3. Wear nothing new. Wear nothing highly starched. Wear nothing with writing on it.

4. Except when limited by circumstance, choose clothing in which you feel comfortable. The more at ease you are, the less likely you'll look out of place. A good detective is as comfortable in a tuxedo as a fatigue jacket. People notice a person who is uncomfortable in his clothes. I know a man who, like a lot of private investigators, is an ex–police officer. He's a good man and a good detective. But he's worthless on

a tail. The moment you see him, you think, "That man is a cop." He looks like a cop because he wears his clothes like a cop. Whatever he wears, he wears like a uniform.

5. Dress for your audience. For example, you shouldn't wear a Hawaiian shirt while tailing a subject in the financial district. Nor should you wear a white shirt and tie when on the boardwalk at the beach.

The primary consideration in choosing your clothes should be the job. Your personal feelings about your appearance, your sense of style, your comfort and ego are all subordinate to the job.

To blend in at the power lunch restaurants and fern bars my subject—a CPA—frequented, I wore a suit and tie every day for a week. I am not fond of a tie. At the end of that week, the subject decided to stop at a bar where I occasionally drink. I gave him a couple of minutes to get settled, then eased into the bar. As I walked in, a friend noticed me. He stared slack-jawed at me for a moment, then stood and pointed me out to his companions. "Look," he said. "It's himself, in a tie." Then he demanded, in a loud drunken voice, to know if I'd been out looking for honest work.

I had to abandon the tail for a few days.

There are times a good detective needs to alter his appearance. The key here is subtlety. Don't try to be a master of disguise. Leave your false whiskers and wig at home, along with your trench coat. The idea is to camouflage yourself, to blend in with your background. A few carefully chosen items of clothing and accessories will suffice. Here are some ideas.

- *Layer your clothing.* Remove and add items sporadically and in different combinations.

- *Glasses.* Alternate between regular glasses and sunglasses. If you don't wear corrective lenses you can often buy frames with clear lenses from optical stores.

- *Hats.* Bring a well-worn baseball cap, one of an unassuming color, without clever sayings. Alternate between wearing it and carrying it. It is unlikely you'll be seen holding it—even in a small crowd people rarely see anything below the shoulders. A beret is compact and can be shoved into the detective's pocket or handbag.

- *Hair.* Women can make startling changes in their appearance simply by undoing a bun (not everything you see in the movies is nonsense).

Occasionally, regardless of how good you are or what precautions you take, you'll find yourself face to face with your subject. Not because you have been burned but because people are unpredictable. Perhaps the subject entered a crowded elevator and you were forced to follow in order to see what floor he got off on. Maybe he was lost in thought, walked past his destination, and suddenly turned around to go back.

When this happens, don't panic. Do something rude. Scratch your crotch or pick your nose, something offensive. When confronted with such behavior, people generally look away. Or at least they avoid looking you in the face. You may lose a little dignity, but dignity is a commodity the working detective cannot afford.

I once tailed a photographer who walked with a pronounced slump in his left shoulder, the result, I assumed, of constantly carrying a heavy camera bag. The slump allowed me to follow him from half a block away on the opposite side of the street. One evening he led me to a notorious gay bar.

I hesitated before following him in. I tried to tell myself I was hesitating because I was afraid of getting burned. I wasn't concerned he'd recognize me in the bar; I was concerned that if he saw my face later on the streets, he might then recognize me.

But the real reason I hesitated was I was afraid. I'd never been in a gay bar. What if somebody I knew saw me going in? What if somebody I knew was already inside?

After a three-minute debate with myself, professionalism won out; I had to go in. I was getting paid, after all, to see what this fellow was up to. Besides, it seemed politically incorrect to worry about the appearance of entering a gay bar. A bar is a bar, I told myself. Spending time in bars is part of the job. How different could a gay bar be?

The answer is, not that different. Aside from the music, which was right out of the forties, and the fact that men (some of whom were in drag) were dancing with other men, it was pretty much like any other bar. In one regard, though, the bar was a detective's dream—there were mirrors everywhere.

I sat on a bar stool near the door, ordered a beer,

and searched the mirrors. But I couldn't spot my photographer. He wasn't sitting at the bar, nor could I see him on the dance floor or at any of the tables.

I'd just about worked up the courage to look for him in one of the rest-rooms (Guys or Dolls?) when I was approached by a man in drag who asked me to dance. I considered it, thinking it would allow me to look for my man without being too conspicuous (how conspicuous can you be dancing with a man in drag?). But I declined. I didn't want to lose my seat by the door and miss seeing my photographer leave.

In the mirror I watched the man in drag turn away to ask somebody else. He had a distinct slump in his left shoulder.

Gender identity may come and go, but posture is forever.

By Car

I saw a television show in which a detective tailed his subject while driving a Ferrari. A bright red Ferrari. It must have stood out like a clown's nose in the subject's rear-view mirror. Despite this obvious handicap, the detective managed to tail his subject all over the island of Hawaii. Ferraris must be common as coconuts in Hawaii, because he never got made.

I have to admit, I'm not that good.

A solo tail in a car is difficult under the best conditions. But to burden yourself with a Ferrari (a burden many of us would gladly suffer) is absurd. It's worse than absurd; it's unprofessional.

A detective should consider the following qualities when selecting a vehicle for tailing:

- *Appearance:* The vehicle should be inconspicuous. Clean without being too shiny; of a common color (blue is the most common, followed by green); free of bumper stickers. And no vanity tags, please. I knew an investigator whose tags spelled SNOOP. They should have spelled STUPID.

- *Performance:* The vehicle should be in good working condition. It should run quietly, without emitting a lot of exhaust fumes or clouds of burning oil. Power is handy; it's not always needed, but on those rare occasions when you tail, say, a subject in a bright red Ferrari, you'll want it.

- *Comfort:* A quality too often overlooked. Detectives spend an inordinate amount of time in their car. Reclining seats are almost mandatory.

At a party, where I'd made a few disparaging remarks about detectives in bright red Ferraris, I was asked what sort of car was best suited for tailing. The answer is easy. A rental car.

Rental cars are wonderful. They come in a variety of colors and sizes and are easily changed, like a steel wardrobe. Just remember to peel off the rental agency decals; they're one more detail that might draw attention.

Preparation

As with tailing on foot, preparation is vital. Plan ahead. Visit the site where you'll begin the tail. If possible, determine the direction the subject is likely to start out in and park your car accordingly. A lot of the stress involved can be alleviated with a few minutes' forethought.

Before beginning the tail make certain you have the following items:

1. Full tank of gas. This detail is so obvious that it sometimes is forgotten.

2. Maps. Get good ones; they're worth the money.

3. Sunglasses. Preferable polarized. It would be stupid to lose your subject because you were squinting into the glare of the sun.

4. Change. Lots of it, for tolls and road drinks.

Plan the excursion as you would a lengthy trip, even if you think you'll only be in the car for thirty minutes.

Familiarize yourself with the car you'll be following. You should, of course, note the make, model, color, year, and license number. But don't stop there. Check for

● Dents and other blemishes
● Bumper stickers
● Antenna arrangement

- Tire tread design (which can be very important when tailing in the country)
- Taillight design, for tailing at night

Always try to learn more than you think you'll need to know. And don't be surprised when that's not enough.

One winter a woman hired me to follow her husband, whom she suspected to be having an affair. She wanted me to find out where he was going after work. I got as much information as I could out of her, including the fact that her husband drove a company truck to and from the plant where he was employed. Although she didn't know the make, model, year, or license number, her description of the vehicle was such that I wasn't worried about missing it. It was a late-model pickup truck (pickups are great—they sit high off the ground, making them easier to spot in traffic) with a company logo on the door. Best of all, she said the truck was painted bright orange.

At 4:45 the next afternoon I was parked near the entrance to the plant waiting. Shortly after 5:00, as the early winter dusk set in, a bright orange pickup with a company logo came out of the gate. It was so bright it looked radioactive. I grinned to myself as I waited for a few shield cars to insert themselves between us. But I didn't grin long. As I started to ease into place, another orange pickup drove out of the plant. And then another. And still another. Seventeen bright orange trucks in all, each with the company logo on the door. I just sat there, feeling like a fool, watching the parade of orange trucks.

Later that night I drove to the client's home with a hammer. Sitting in the drive was her husband's bright orange pickup. I parked half a block away, took out the hammer, walked quietly back to her house, and smashed the truck's left taillight. The next afternoon, when the legion of bright orange trucks emerged, only one had a shattered left taillight. The rest was easy.

Well, as easy as it ever gets.

Tactics

There is one major advantage to tailing by car over tailing by foot. A car is confining. Your subject can't suddenly decide to step into a doorway, or walk down the up escalator. Everywhere your subject goes, he has to take a ton of steel with him. Cars are unwieldy. They limit where your subject can go. Traffic laws can also work in your favor. Fortunately, most people obey most of the rules of the road. A detective on a solo tail dreads the thought of an illegal U-turn.

Unfortunately, those same limitations also apply to you. In a car you're unable to respond as quickly or as subtly as on foot. Nor can you violate traffic laws without risking notice, of either the subject or the police. The same laws that prevent your subject from making U-turns allow him to turn right on a red light, leaving you to pound your steering wheel in frustration.

There are two related elements that demand constant attention while engaged in a solo tail.

1. Shield cars
2. Distance

These, in turn, are dependent on external conditions, such as—

1. Traffic density
2. Traffic speed and flow
3. Weather
4. Lighting conditions

You have limited control over the first two elements, none over the rest. Once again it's you versus a random universe.

Shield cars are vehicles you allow between yourself and your subject. The number of shield cars depends on external conditions and your self-confidence. For example, you can allow more shield cars on an interstate highway, where exits are limited and fewer surprises can happen. Conversely, in dense city traffic you'll want fewer shield cars (perhaps only one or two) between yourself and your subject.

Too many shield cars makes it extremely difficult to maintain visual contact with your subject and increases the odds of losing him. Too few shield cars increases the odds of getting burned. Distance is more of a factor when there are few or no shield cars, such as in the country or in the city during early-morning hours. Maintaining appropriate distance works much the same way. During bad weather and at night, tighten up the distance between yourself and your subject.

Oddly enough, people who drive too fast are easier to follow than those who drive too slow. Speeders are paying attention to the road, looking for openings in traffic, and watching for cops. Loafers disrupt traffic and spend a lot of time glancing fearfully in the rear-view mirror.

The toughest tail I ever conducted was of an old woman, the grandmother I mentioned in Chapter 1. As I said, I wasn't interested in her, but in her grandson, with whom she was very close. I was watching her in the hope that she'd lead me to him.

The woman drove everywhere; six blocks to the market, eight blocks to the post office. And she rarely drove faster than 25 miles per hour. That wouldn't have been a problem except that most of the streets in her neighborhood were four lanes—two in each direction—and the speed limit was 45. One car driving 25 in a 45 zone stands out; two cars looks like a small funeral. It couldn't be done subtly. Eventually I switched to a bicycle and followed her from the sidewalks.

It worked, by the way. I found the kid.

Summary

At first tailing can seem intimidating. There is so much that is beyond your control, so much that can go wrong. The first time I conducted a solo tail, I was a nervous wreck. I lost the subject within a few blocks. How can anybody ever do this? I wondered.

Well, like this:

1. Prepare. Learn as much as you possible can, but accept that it may not be enough.

2. Plan ahead. From the beginning control all

the factors you can. Give some thought to those you can't control, but don't focus too much on them.

3. Pay attention. Be aware of what is taking place around you, but don't get bogged down in details.

4. Relax. When you get too anxious, you make mistakes.

5. Know when to quit. Perseverance is good; stubbornness is not. Don't blow a tail because you're too tired or irritated to do a good job.

Tailing is perhaps the toughest skill a detective has to learn. Often, it's the most rewarding. It's certainly the most fun. And, with practice and patience, you can do it.

But, if you do it, if you choose to tail somebody, make certain you have a good reason. This is not something you do for amusement. There are laws against harassment (see Chapter 10). If you make the decision to conduct a tail, then do it right. Do it in a professional manner. The job comes first. Always. Not your temper, not your comfort, not your ego. The job.

Chapter 3

WATCHING AND WAITING

THE QUIET CRAFT OF SURVEILLANCE

As much as I love my work, there are times when I don't want to be a lawyer. I want to be something else. When that happens, I talk Greg into letting me go out on an investigation with him. I learn something new, and the experience makes me appreciate my own job more.

On one such occasion I convinced Greg to let me serve a subpoena. It was for a woman who had listened to the man in the next apartment beat his wife for nearly two years. One day, after the man had left the apartment, the wife set their bed on fire. Unfortunately, a good part of the apartment house burned along with the bed. The wife was charged with arson.

The woman was needed to testify the following day about the battering. We went to the woman's new apartment and I knocked on the door. She answered and I explained that I had a subpoena for her. I hadn't even finished talking when she slammed the door in my face. After recovering from the shock, I knocked again, but she refused to answer.

I was angry. How dare that woman shut the door in

my face. I wanted to serve that subpoena more than anything. So, very early the next morning, Greg and I staked out the apartment house. We were waiting for the woman to come out and go to work. As she left the building, we'd nail her with the subpoena. I had to be there, because I was the only person who would recognize her. I was jazzed. A stake-out.

But we just sat there. And sat there. And sat there. Greg sort of slumped down and became part of the car seat. But I was going nuts. Where was she? What was she doing? What if she decided not to go to work that day? What if I missed her? Why wasn't Greg as nervous as I was? He just sat there, like nothing was going on. Bastard. Where in the hell was she?

I swear we waited for nearly two hours before she finally came out. Greg says it was closer to forty minutes.

Maybe I've got the wrong attitude.

R.G.

Stake-out. The phrase has sort of a gritty, sexy ring to it, doesn't it? Maybe that's why private detectives don't use it. We know better.

We usually call it surveillance. That term is gritty enough, but not very alluring. And that's a pretty accurate description of the job. Lots of grit, no allure.

Essentially, surveillance is the craft of seeing without being seen. At its worst, and it is most commonly at its worst, it can be mind-numbingly dull. At its best, surveillance can be oddly exciting. Not thrilling, but stimulating in a quiet, warped way.

Surveillance is most often done in conjunction with tailing. You need to scrutinize the activities of a certain person, so you follow him and watch him. Tailing and surveillance go together like chicken fried steak and cream gravy.

In some cases, however, you are more interested in a place than a person. For example, you may want to identify the people who enter a certain office or apartment. On other occasions the place may be simply a link to the person you're interested in. Once, while trying to find a man who was avoiding a subpoena, I set up a surveillance on his lover and waited for him to show up. Only took about three hours.

There are basically two aspects to surveillance: external and internal. The external aspect has to do with the active techniques, the methods for "casing" a location, the use of alternate spotting locations, the act of observation itself.

The internal aspect has to do with the way the detective works the surveillance mentally, the way he prepares himself and deals with the demand that he be tirelessly observant. This aspect is normally the most difficult for the detective, the beginner and the old hand as well.

For example, I was assisting another investigator in a surveillance and tail. I'd never worked with this man before, but he had several years' more experience than I did and I'd heard a lot about him. I was looking forward to learning from the experience.

The subject was a man who was having an affair with one of the client's daughters. The client felt the man was a playboy and a scoundrel and wasn't pleased with the thought of him with his baby girl. He also believed the man was sleeping with other women, and he'd hired the investigator to confirm his suspicions.

On the first evening of the assignment, we met near the subject's office at four o'clock in the afternoon. My partner parked his car in a position where he could see both the subject's office and his car. I took a position across the street in the parking lot of a small shopping mall. We had two-way radios but.

after making a radio check to ensure the sets were functioning properly, we decided not to use them until the subject was moving. People tend to take notice of men in cars speaking into walkie-talkies. The last thing either of us wanted was to attract attention.

Since my role was secondary—I wouldn't be needed until the subject began to move—I didn't settle into my normal surveillance mode. Instead I listened to the car radio and thumbed through a magazine. By five-thirty I was beginning to get impatient. By six o'clock I was cursing the subject for working so late. I hate an overachiever. By six-thirty I began to wonder if my partner had let the subject slip. I decided to break radio silence and find out what, if anything, was going on. So I flipped on the radio. No answer from my partner.

I sat there for a moment, thinking of all the things that could have gone wrong. My radio could have malfunctioned. Or *his* radio could have malfunctioned. Who knows, there could have been heavy sunspot activity that interfered with the radio transmission.

In the end I decided it didn't matter. What mattered was that my partner had probably signaled me and I hadn't heard. I was certain that while I was listening to the radio and catching up on the news of the day, the subject had driven off with my poor partner in pursuit, wondering what the hell had happened to me.

Before giving it up entirely, I decided to make a quick check of the office parking lot. I got out of my car and walked across the street to check. There, in the otherwise empty parking lot, was the other investigator's car. He was slumped over in it, sound asleep. And snoring. It sounded like a chain saw.

I didn't wake him. I just stuck a note under his windshield wiper: GET A JOB.

In surveillance the internal and external aspects must work in coordination. They are absolutely dependent on each other. Being well prepared or being in the right spot is no help if you're napping while the action takes place.

External Aspects

There are only three components to surveillance: the preparation, the surveillance itself, and the breaking off. Remember, the whole point is to see without being seen. If you prepare properly, work it properly, and break off properly, your subject will never know you were there.

Preparation

As with all facets of detective work, preparation is the first consideration. Since surveillance is usually done in conjunction with tailing, many of the same preparatory steps are required. In addition, the following steps should be taken:

1. Case the site.

2. Dress appropriately.

3. Be well rested.

4. Have the proper equipment.

5. Bring a snack.

These are common-sense steps. I mention them because it's amazing how frequently people fail to use their common sense.

1. Case the site. This isn't always possible. There will be times when you tail somebody to an unfamiliar place and have to set up an impromptu surveillance. When that happens, all you can do is improvise.

But if you can case the site, do it. Visit the site at a quiet hour. Find all the exits. Identify alternative spotting locations and consider how quickly you can shift between them without breaking surveillance. Pay attention to details—street lamps, traffic conditions, and the like.

2. Dress appropriately. If possible, wear clothing that fits the circumstances. See the section on clothing in the previous chapter.

You want to be comfortable as well as inconspicuous. Most surveillances are conducted from a car. While that offers some protection from the elements, it doesn't help much during extremely hot or cold weather. The only thing more miserable than sweltering in a car on an airless summer day is freezing in that same car in the middle of January. You're supposed to be inconspicuous, remember? So you can't run your car's heater or air conditioner. A running car might attract attention. This is especially true in the winter when the exhaust is so visible.

The worst surveillance I ever conducted took place

in the winter in New England. Winters in New England can be savage. I had to be at the site at 5:00 A.M., which may be the most dismal hour on the clock. I wore long underwear, two pair of wool socks, a flannel shirt, a bulky sweater, all under a snowmobile suit. I was so cumbersome in that outfit that I could barely bend my leg enough to apply the brakes. It was just barely enough to keep me warm. It was just about perfect, in other words. If I had been any warmer, I'd probably have fallen asleep. Any colder and I'd probably be missing a few fingers and toes right now.

3. Be well rested. Try to get plenty of sleep before beginning the surveillance. Or bring along something to compensate for it. You may need to be awake and alert for a very long time. No Doz and related products can help you extend your effective hours, although you pay for it later.

4. Have the proper equipment. Binoculars or a spotting scope are often useful during surveillance. Sound amplification devices, such as the small dish antennae you see on the sidelines of football games, can be extremely handy. And if you're going to be taking photographs, make sure you have the proper lenses and film of the appropriate speed. Make sure that the batteries for any electronic equipment are working and that you have spare ones just in case. This isn't rocket science, but equipment failure at the wrong time could be disastrous.

5. Bring a snack. Food is important. You don't burn a lot of calories while conducting a surveillance, but you need to keep hunger at bay in order to rid yourself of the distraction.

Trail mix is the ideal snoop snack. It's a conglomeration of nuts, raisins, M & M's, cereal, and just about anything else that won't melt. It's good source of quick energy and doesn't spoil.

To drink, a little tea or coffee is good. The key phrase, though, is *a little*. Too much fluid can lead to calamity. A Thermos of ice chips is good for the summer. Ice chips keep you from getting too thirsty without filling you with fluid.

I make these recommendations based on experience. One of my first cases as a detective involved the surveillance of a doctor's office. My client wanted to know if a certain person was seeing the doctor. The reasons for his curiosity aren't relevant now; all you need to know is that I was hired to watch a specific office for a specific person on a specific day.

I hadn't conducted a prolonged surveillance before, but I'd discussed it with other detectives and thought I could handle the situation. The evening before the actual surveillance I drove to the doctor's office, parked nearby, and made a foot reconnaissance of the area. I noticed the office had entrances in the front and on the side. Both entrances were visible from the street. I also found three or four good secondary spotting locations.

The next morning I was at the doctor's office by 7:00 A.M., a full two hours before it opened. I had my choice of parking spaces and chose one where I could see both entrances clearly.

I was both nervous and excited. I was being a real detective, doing real detective stuff. I loved it. For the first hour.

I was totally unprepared for how tedious a surveillance can be. The first hour seemed to flash by. The second hour was a little slower, and the third seemed positively sluggish.

Not knowing how long I'd have to wait for the subject to arrive, I'd brought along enough food and drink for nine or ten hours. I figured the food would help me remain alert. Instead, it was distracting. I kept thinking about it. And even worse, the thought of all that food made me unnaturally hungry. By 11:00 A.M., less than four hours after beginning the surveillance, I'd decided I should eat a little of the food, just so I wouldn't be so distracted by it. By noon I'd eaten all the food and drunk most of the milk and soda.

Around one o'clock, I began to feel the need to relieve myself. This *never* happened to detectives in the movies. I couldn't leave—what if the person arrived while I was searching for a rest-room? On the other hand, I didn't relish the idea of wetting my pants.

I got out of the car, thinking a little activity would take my mind off my bladder. I spent the next hour coasting among the spotting locations I'd noted the night before. I couldn't stand still. The need was becoming urgent.

By 2:30 my bladder felt like it was the size of a soccer ball. I was certain it would rupture and I'd die of septicemia, if that's what it is you die from when your bladder explodes. Whatever it's called, it's *not* how detectives are supposed to die.

Finally, driven by desperation and unable to think of a better solution, I got back into the car, unfolded an empty milk carton, and urinated into it. You have to be both nimble and patient to urinate into a milk carton while sitting in a car on a public street. Nimble, patient, and desperate.

It might have been worth it if the subject had ever appeared. She never did.

The Surveillance Itself

The actual act of surveillance is simple. You just watch and pay attention. anybody with decent eyesight can do it. In fact, anybody with eyesight correctable by lenses can do it. All you have to do is observe. It's simple.

The trick, however, is to see without being seen. It's not as difficult as it sounds. It just requires a little thought.

Here are some things to consider:

1. Surveillance methods

2. Spotting locations

3. Concealment

If you pay attention and apply your common sense to these matters, you shouldn't have any problems. We'll examine each item in turn.

Surveillance Methods There are three basic methods of surveillance:

- From a vehicle
- On foot
- From a building

Most surveillance is done from a parked vehicle.

This has a great many advantages. You're protected from the elements, you're instantly prepared to tail your subject, any equipment you might need is handy, and the vehicle provides partial concealment.

On the other hand, vehicles are large and unwieldy, which limits you mainly to streets and parking lots. And while you may be protected from rain, sleet, hail, snow, and wind, you aren't protected from excessive heat in the summer and extreme cold in the winter. Remember, you can't use the heater or the air conditioner without being conspicuous.

Occasionally a surveillance will be conducted on foot. This is usually the case when the object of the surveillance is located away from a public road. I know a team of detectives who followed their subject on a camping trip. They tailed him in a canoe and camped a half-mile away. When they returned, they were covered with mosquito bites and ridden with ticks. But they had the evidence they needed.

Foot surveillance isn't limited to such extreme circumstances. I sometimes alternate between vehicle and foot surveillance. It breaks the monotony and allows me to stretch cramped muscles.

A foot surveillance has the advantage of allowing movement. In addition, it tends to keep detectives more alert and gives them more freedom in selecting spotting locations.

However, a foot surveillance greatly limits the amount of equipment available to you. A person carrying field glasses on a city street is likely to attract attention, even in New York or Chicago. Being afoot also leaves you ill prepared for a quick exit, should the subject decide to leave suddenly.

On occasion, a surveillance will be conducted from

a building. This could be a public building, such as a diner, or a private one, such as an empty office or a motel room. Generally, this type of surveillance is most useful when you are interested in a specific place rather than in a specific person.

For example, during a divorce case, I had to conduct a surveillance on a small, suburban bungalow. My client's husband was a motorcycle enthusiast, and with her financial help, he'd purchased and restored four old motorcycles. However, when discussing the property settlement, he claimed the motorcycles had all been stolen. All four of them. His wife suspected he was storing them in a buddy's garage. The suburban bungalow.

I tried a number of scams to get a peek into the garage, none of which I care to mention here. In any event, all of them failed. However, I'd noticed a house for sale across the street and a couple houses down from the bungalow, but still offering a good view of the garage. I called on the realtor, showed him my detective's license, and gave him a moderately accurate idea of what I was doing, without revealing which house I was interested in. He was intrigued by the cloak-and-dagger aspect of my activities and let me use the house.

It was great. A house has enormous advantages in that you are usually less physically restricted, you are spared any struggle with the weather, and you have access to the facility most coveted by detectives—a toilet.

I was only there for about thirty hours when the owner of the bungalow opened the garage door and gave me the chance to take some lovely photographs of two gleaming motorcycles. The photos were enough to pry the location of the other motorcycles from the husband and to convince him to be somewhat more generous in the property settlement.

There are occasions when I'll use a restaurant, bar, or diner as a secondary spotting location. Obviously, you must have a table beside a window. If you order food, order a cheeseburger or some other common item, one that won't require long preparation. And be prepared to pay in cash. You may not have time to deal with charge cards. Don't pay at the register, even if it means leaving an obscenely large tip. Remember, every minute you spend away from the surveillance you could be missing something.

Spotting Locations A spotting location is the place from which you conduct the surveillance. There are both primary and secondary spotting locations. The primary location is where you'll spend most of your time. If possible, it should be selected before beginning the surveillance. It should be close enough to the object of the surveillance for you to see it plainly, but far enough away that you aren't obvious.

Secondary locations are those that aren't quite as good as the primary one, but allow the detective to shift around from place to place. Usually I look for secondary locations that get me out of the car. A diner with a convenient window, for example, or a stoop where rummies hang out.

It's also helpful to have a secondary parking location. This can be risky, however, in that you can't focus your attention on the object of surveillance while you're moving your car. Every minute you shift your attention from the object increases the chance that you'll miss something important.

Good spotting locations are difficult to find in the suburbs. Suburbanites tend to notice strange vehicles in their neighborhood and are more willing to notify the police. I try to park my car near the property line between two houses. That way people at each house tend to think the car is somehow connected with the other house.

Concealment When conducting a surveillance from my car, I recline the seat until I can just see above the dashboard. I usually wear a baseball cap which I pull down to conceal my eyes. Then I sit very still. If a passer-by notices me, he thinks I'm napping. Oddly enough, people rarely seem to notice. I've parked on busy streets, in convenience-store and restaurant parking lots, even in the driveways of group houses, without being noticed.

I'm convinced that sitting very still is the key to escaping notice in a car. Movement attracts attention. You'll learn more about this in the section on the internal aspects of surveillance.

On foot, you can escape notice by blending in with the other people on the street. Unlike surveillance from a car, you can't stay still very long on foot. Merchants in the area tend to notice loiterers and get suspicious. That could mean a visit by the police, wondering what you're up to.

The only exception to this is if you can find a natural way to avoid notice. On more than one occasion I've bought a pint of vodka and joined a group of rummies on the street (they get the pint; I drink soda out of a paper bag). They're always glad to get a pint and are good cover. People actively avoid looking directly at homeless people and drunks.

Breaking Off

Deciding when to terminate a surveillance is a judgment call. It depends entirely on the situation. And since no two situations are ever the same, I can't give you any solid rules about when to break off. But I can give you some general guidelines.

Break off the surveillance—

1. If you think you might have been made. You can always try again. The O'Hara rule—tomorrow is another day—applies here.

2. If you've attracted any sort of unwanted attention, or if a disturbance happens nearby. A cop questioning you about loitering, for example, or maybe some street person panhandling nearby. Even if you don't think your subject noticed, don't take the chance. Better safe than sorry, if you'll pardon the cliché.

3. About an hour after you're absolutely certain your subject is in for the night.

4. When you feel the risk is too high. Any sort of risk—the risk of getting made, the risk of getting mugged, the risk of falling asleep.

Obviously, you should also break off a surveillance if you actually *have* been made.

Use your common sense. Unless you are under the pressure of a deadline, or unless you think something critical is about to happen, don't take any unwarranted chances. Break off and try again later.

On the other hand, don't be overly timid. He is not worthy of the honeycomb that shuns the hive because the bees have stings. That was Shakespeare's way of saying got no guts, get no glory.

As I said, breaking off is always a judgment call.

If you think there's a chance your subject might leave after you've broken off the surveillance, put a cheap watch under a tire on the subject's car. When he drives away, he'll smash the watch. You can recover the watch in the morning. The hands of the watch will tell you what time the subject left.

I actually learned that trick from the movie *Chinatown*. It's the only practical investigative technique I've ever seen on film. I haven't had the occasion to use it yet, but I believe it will work. Besides, it's such a great scam I have to pass it along.

Just be certain you *don't* use a digital watch.

Internal Aspects

When conducting a surveillance, you may be required to watch a certain location for hours without respite. During that time you cannot allow yourself to be distracted, either by some nearby activity or through tedium. You may have to disregard weariness, to distance yourself from your bodily needs.

You may need to ignore discomfort, bug bites, muscle cramps, headaches, anything that might divert your attention.

How is that done?

Of all the factors influencing the success of a surveillance, the mental process is the most demanding. It's also the hardest to discuss. For a group whose livelihood depends on the ability to observe, analyze, and explain, detectives are remarkably nonintrospective. They seldom indulge in self-examination.

I've asked other detectives how they manage to stay alert despite everything. I always get vague answers. "I don't know; I just *do* it."

I can try to tell you how I do it. Maybe it'll help you. Maybe not.

I disconnect my brain from my body. I let my body drift away until it no longer seems to be connected to me.

Sound ridiculous? It sounds that way to me, too. But that's what I do. I position the car, lean the seat back to the point where my eyes are at a level with the dashboard, and pull my cap down to conceal my eyes. Then I shut down all unnecessary systems.

I find I become very aware of what's going on around me, but I feet totally unaffected by it. I see people walking, I notice the cars driving by, I hear airplanes flying over head. It's as if my mind is connected and my body is detached.

It took me a while to develop this ability, if that's what it is. At first I had to consciously relax my body. First the feet, then the legs, and so on. Now my body seems to relax on its own. Except for my tongue.

Every hour or so I'm surprised to find my tongue has jammed itself against the roof of my mouth.

I know this process sounds vaguely mystical. I feel foolish writing it down. But it works for me. And so I don't question it very much.

There you have it. The *tao* of surveillance.

Chapter 4

THE PAPER TRAIL

I represented an eighteen-year-old boy accused of vandalizing a car. The car, a Corvette, belonged to another teenager, a high school classmate of my client. This kid had stolen the heart of the girl my client loved. My client blamed it on the car. He felt she would have been true to him, except for the Corvette. How could she resist a Corvette?

So one fine spring day I was in court with my client, facing a charge of malicious mischief, to wit: throwing black paint and sand on a 1978 Corvette, license number PRQ229. The prosecution's case was fairly short. The victim testified that my client had no authority to throw paint and sand onto his car and explained that he was dating my client's former girlfriend. The arresting officer testified that he'd decided to interview my client after the victim told him about the girlfriend situation. During the interview, he'd noticed black paint spattered on my client's shoes.

I called only one witness. A man from the Department of Motor Vehicles. He brought a certified copy of the registration for the car that had been issued license number PRQ229. The registration was for a 1977 Dodge. My client was not charged with vandalizing a 1977 Dodge. The judge dismissed the case.

What had happened? Was this just another bureaucratic blunder? Not quite. The victim had sold his 1977 Dodge when he bought the Corvette. But he kept the license plate and put it on his new car. And he didn't notify the Department of Motor Vehicles. Why? Who knows why an eighteen-year-old kid does anything?

We came across the discrepancy by accident. Greg was doing what he calls the grunt work, checking all the dreary details, following the paper trail. But in this case the paper trail was the Yellow Brick Road. It didn't lead to Oz, but it kept my client out of jail.

Unfortunately for him, he still lost the girl.

R.G.

Information is the detective's stock in trade. That's one of the reasons people turn to detectives—for information they either can't, or don't know how to, find themselves. How do detectives do it? Through the knowledge and development of information sources.

In this chapter you'll learn about the detective's information-gathering techniques. You'll learn how to establish and nurture personal sources, and how to find your way through the maze of official documents. You'll also learn some tips on the etiquette of bribery. In addition, I'll give you a practical demonstration showing how easily you can gather a great deal of information about practically anybody.

Most information sources fit into one of two categories:

- Personal: information possessed by people.

- Archival: written information; from books, files, official records and the like.

A good detective needs to be familiar with both.

Personal Sources

It is much more difficult to extract information from people than from documents. If the information exists on paper, all it takes is knowing where to look and having the patience to do the looking.

People are more complicated. They may have information you want, but be unwilling to share it with you. They may have the information and not even know it. Or they may not have the information, but they know where you can get it.

In a later chapter I'll cover the techniques of interviewing. In this chapter I want to show you how to cultivate people in certain information-rich positions—bartenders, police officers, clerks, telephone operators, to name a few. These are all sources of valuable information, information that is tough to get anywhere else. The difficulty is getting them to give it to you.

How do you do it? You nurture a relationship with them. You make an effort to know them, to show some interest in them, to care about them. It's very odd; when you make that effort, you often find you actually do come to care about these people.

People respond to genuine interest. They tell you things, or help you find the information you want, or point you in the right direction.

I recall having to interview eight or nine nurses for a criminal case. They worked different shifts and in different departments. It would have taken me weeks to catch them all. But I'd taken the time on a previous case to be friendly with the nursing supervisor. I'd sent her a thank-you note after the case was over, and a letter to her supervisor praising her for her assistance. Since she remembered me, she arranged for all the nurses to be at the hospital at a specific time and provided me with an office where I could speak to them individually.

Cultivating relationships can make the difference between success and failure. How is it done? Like this. Let's say you want to establish a relationship with a records clerk in city hall and a bartender at a local pub. There are four steps you need to consider:

1. Your purpose.
2. Your target.
3. Their usual audience.
4. Your approach.

I realize this sounds cold-blooded. It is cold-blooded. But the fact that you have an ulterior motive when you approach these people does not preclude your learning to like them. And if it turns out, after you've cultivated their friendship, that you *don't* like them—well, it's a cold-blooded business. Get used to it.

1. *Consider your purpose.* Why do you need to cultivate a friendship with a clerk in city hall? Why a bartender in that particular bar?

The clerk may work in the tax assessor's office. Although there is a great deal of public information there, the clerks are often too busy, or unwilling, to help you with it. A friend in the tax assessor's office can save you a lot of time. A bonus is that city hall staff often know each other. A clerk in one department is often familiar with clerks in other departments. A friendly introduction can get you places you couldn't reach on your own.

The bartender? Let's say he works at a trendy bar, one where people go to meet and discuss business. A bartender who knows who is talking to whom, or who is sleeping with whom, can be a valuable asset.

2. *Consider your audience.* What sort of person is likely to become a clerk in city hall? The job is usually poorly paid and often monotonous. In other words, it's the kind of job women are so often forced to take. We can safely assume the clerk is a woman. She could be any age, but is likely to be married. She is probably as overworked as she is underpaid. Her feet probably hurt and she is worried about gaining weight, but still takes pride in her appearance. She quietly resents being thought of as a mere extension of the typewriter.

The bartender, on the other hand, is probably male. He likes people, or he wouldn't have become a bartender. He's probably young, but likes to think he is wise in the ways of a wicked world. He's likely to be somewhat self-centered and arrogant. Since he's working in a trendy bar, he probably likes money and the fast life.

3. *Consider their usual audience.* The people most clerks face are in a hurry. They want something and they want it *now*. They're often rude, demanding, and impatient. A clerk, to them, is a manifestation of a mindless, malevolent bureaucracy. They treat her like a semi-intelligent and uncooperative stamp machine.

The bartender's audience is somewhat different. The people are usually pleasanter, but still tend to treat the bartender as a sort of servant. Despite their moneyed status they often leave little or no tip. They have no idea how difficult it is to run an efficient bar, how tough it is to handle unruly customers without a scene.

4. *Consider your approach.* Let them grow accustomed to your smiling face. Go to city hall fairly often. If you don't actually need anything, pretend you do. Always chat with the clerk for a while. It doesn't matter what you chat about—the weather, children, anything uncontroversial—all that matters is that you are patient and pleasant. Clerks rarely see pleasant faces. Always thank her for her help, even if she didn't actually provide any.

Do the same at the bar. Go there often, but go before it gets crowded. Don't sit at a table, take a stool at the bar. You don't have to drink a lot; you don't have to drink at all. Order a club soda with a twist of lime—the bartender will think you're on the wagon. Chat with him. Don't interrogate him, or quiz him. Just have a simple chat. Talk about sports or ask about the bar. Or just shake your head and say, "Boy, I bet you've seen some things working here." If he's not busy, he's likely to tell you bar stories. All bartenders have bar stories; most of them are worth listening to. Leave him a gracious tip when you leave. Not an ostentatious tip, but a somewhat generous one.

As you can see, it takes time to cultivate a worthwhile relationship. But in the long run it usually makes the job easier and gives you access to information you couldn't ordinarily get.

Once you've cultivated a source, you don't have to go back as often. But you must still visit occasionally. They have to see your friendly face.

I make rounds, like a doctor. Every three to five weeks, I take an evening and visit a number of bars. I make sure the bartender sees my face, even if I don't talk with him. I order a beer, take a few sips, leave a good tip, and go to the next bar.

I do the same with all my sources. It's like maintaining your car. You change the oil every three months.

Remember, all these clerks and secretaries and mechanics and bartenders are important. These people run the world. If they don't do their job, everything comes to a crashing halt. Treat them as if they're important. They'll remember you and like you. And they'll help you.

There are no guarantees, of course. Sometimes all the charm and friendliness in the world won't get you where you want to be. What then?

Bribery.

There's an old saying: Money talks; bullshit walks. Like so many old sayings, it's only partially accurate. Bullshit is almost always enough. But there are times when the judicious application of cash can work wonders.

Bribery of public officials—and a records clerk could be considered a public official—is a crime. I have to advise you not to commit a crime. But on those occasions when an offer to make a person's pockets a little heavier is appropriate, here are a few simple rules:

1. *Be discreet*. Without fanfare and without

looking at it, put the money where your target can see it and reach it.

2. *Don't mention the money.* Say something like, "I really need this information." Your target will know what the money is for.

3. *Don't be cheap.* This is not time to consider economics. Offering any bill less than a twenty is an insult. Think in terms of multiple twenties and fifties.

4. *Don't gloat.* If your target takes the cash, don't let that "I knew you could be bought" look cross your face.

5. *Accept a refusal gracefully.* Smile shamefacedly. Then get the hell out of there.

I realize this is a little sordid. And it's my experience that a good detective rarely needs to resort to crossing palms. But let's not be naive. And if you decide you have to do it, do it right.

Archival Sources

There are only two requirements for finding archival data: knowing where to look, and patience. I can't teach you to be patient. But I *can* show you where to look.

In the back of this book is a list of the major sources of archival information and the kinds of information that can be obtained from each source. What I'll do in this section is give you an idea of how the search for archival data is conducted.

Archival trails come in two varieties:

- Personal: the public information available on people.
- Property: the public information available on property.

I'll introduce you to both.

The Personal Trail

The best way to learn a thing is by doing it. You can't learn to ride a bicycle by following instructions in a book. Learning to follow a trail of public information is much easier than learning to ride a bicycle, but the same principle applies.

I'm going to give you an assignment (if it helps, think of it as a case). Then I'll walk you through a similar hypothetical case. The investigation we're going to make shouldn't take more than eight hours if you schmooze the clerks properly.

> *Assignment:* OPEN YOUR TELEPHONE BOOK AT RANDOM. PICK A NAME. FIND OUT EVERYTHING YOU CAN ABOUT THIS PERSON.

Don't panic. I'm going to show you what to do. This isn't going to be as difficult as it sounds. Trust me. When you're done, you'll be surprised at how easy it was.

All the material we gather is going to be public information. Although it is collected and stored by various state and local bodies, the information is there for you. But you have to ask for it. Sometimes you have to remind those in charge of the data that they're obligated to give it to you. But it's yours by right.

Here we go. We open the telephone book and this is what we see:

DOE, JOHN 1234 ADAMS ST..................................**123-4567**

Not very original, I grant you, but it will do for our purposes.

Our first step is the library. On the way we drive by 1234 Adams Street to look at John Doe's home. It's a small ranch-style house in a quiet, working-class neighborhood. The yard is neat and we can see a chain-link fence enclosing the back yard.

At the library we ask for the city directory. Every city, and most towns, have a book called the city directory. This is not a telephone book. It's a book published by a private company. The city directory cross-indexes the city's residents by name, address, and telephone number. If Mr. Doe has been living in the city for a while, he will probably be listed. The listing will look something like this:

DOE, JOHN S (STEPHANIE, R, PERKINS HARDWARE)
4ⓗ
CALEDONIA ENTERPRISES 1234 ADAMS ST. 123-4567

This tells you John Doe is employed at Caledonia Enterprises. He is married to Stephanie R. Doe, who works at Perkins Hardware. There are four people living at his address—presumably John, Stephanie, and two children. The circle with the letter h in it indicates Doe owns, or is buying, the house at 1234 Adams Street.

The city directory increased our knowledge of

John Doe only marginally. But it gives us a base of information on which we can build. It widens the area of search.

Our next stop is city hall. At the motor vehicle department we ask the clerk to check for automobiles registered to either John or Stephanie Doe. We learn John Doe drives a blue 1987 Chevy Blazer, license number 32390A3. Stephanie drives a yellow 1985 Toyota Corolla, with a vanity license plate reading STEVIE. We also learn John owns a 17-foot Boston Whaler (boats have to be licensed in most states).

Down the hall at the tax assessor's office (the tax assessor determines the value of property and imposes a property tax) we ask the clerk for the records regarding Mr. Doe's property. The information may be listed either by the address or by the name of the person paying the tax. We find out that the house at 1234 Adams Street is listed under John Doe's name. An assessed value is recorded for the property. (Don't confuse the assessed value of a property with its full market value. Assessed value is usually a quarter to a half of market value. The assessment factor either will be listed or can be determined by asking a clerk.) Any unpaid property taxes will also be noted. John has paid his property taxes. No other property is listed to either John or Stephanie.

At the voter registration office we ask to see the voter registration card for both John and Stephanie. John is registered as a Democrat, while his wife is an Independent. The card also lists their birthdays. John was born January 4, 1940; Stephanie was born the following year on August 13.

Our picture of John Doe is beginning to fill out. We know he is married and has a family. It's reasonable to guess that he and his wife bring home a moderately comfortable income from their jobs since they own two cars and a boat, as well as their house. We can speculate they have two children. And we can safely assume Stephanie prefers to be called Stevie.

Next we go to the county courthouse. At the marriage license section of the county recorder's office (or in the office of vital statistics), we ask the clerk for John and Stevie's application for a marriage license. We learn John Doe and Stephanie Roe were married on July 12, 1962. The marriage certificate also tells us the names and addresses of John and Stevie's parents, as well as their mothers' maiden names. We also get a look at both John and Stevie's signatures. The names of the witnesses, who were probably either relatives or very good friends, are also listed.

At the same office, in the birth certificate section, we look to see if any children were born to Stevie. We find Peter Doe was born 1/21/63. His sister, Theresa, was born 6/2/65.

At the county clerk's civil office we ask the clerk if either John or Stevie has been involved in any lawsuits, and whether any liens have been placed on their property. None are recorded. We do learn, however, that John was married once before—to Alice Desmaris. They were divorced in 1959.

At the criminal section of the county clerk's office we ask if either John or Stevie has any criminal charges pending, or if they have ever been indicted or tried for a crime in the past. Once again, there is no record of any such involvement.

Our next stop at the courthouse is the office of the county recorder (sometimes called the register of deeds). This is where all property transactions taking place in the county are recorded. The county recorder keeps an index book listing the names of those who have purchased or sold property. The index is by calendar year. The person who sold the property is referred in the index, and on the deed, as the grantor. The person who purchased the property is called the grantee.

By searching under John Doe's name in each yearly index we learn that he purchased the house at 1234 Adams Street in 1963. We also learn how much the property cost and who he bought it from. He had a twenty-year mortgage with the First National Bank.

Our final stop is the probate office. Although we assume John and Stevie Doe are still alive, we can check on their parents (remember, we found their names on the marriage license). Nothing is recorded for Stevie's family, but we discover John's father died in November of 1962, leaving him a tidy sum.

In three stops we've learned a great deal about John Doe, and we can conjecture more. We know John was married and divorced at the age of nineteen. We know he remarried and can guess that his second marriage may have been hastened by Stevie becoming pregnant (check the dates). We can further guess that John's inheritance from his father allowed him to make a down payment on the house, an uncommon extravagance for most young newlyweds expecting a baby.

Can we learn more? Of course. We don't know a thing about his employment history, or any medical problems, or his credit rating. We don't even know what he looks like. Does he have hobbies? Does he drink? And after we know all those things, there will be still more to learn, and more after that.

In order to obtain a more complete picture of John Doe, we have to go beyond the paper trail. We have to interview people—his neighbors, his co-workers, his former employers (interviewing techniques are covered in another chapter). We'd also be wise to examine Doe's trash (also covered in another chapter).

The best way to learn to find your way through the sea of public information is to wade in and swim. You'll probably be nervous the first time you approach a clerk in city hall and ask for information about a total stranger. I was. But, as I said, it's public information. You have a right to it. Some clerks, especially those in smaller towns, may not know the information is public. They may give you a hard time, but you have the right. It's up to you to exercise it.

Property Trail

There is nothing sexy about following the property trail. It is dull, tedious work. It can also be vitally important.

There are two kinds of property—real and personal. Personal property is the stuff you own, cars and refrigerators, and such. Real property means land and buildings. We're only concerned with real property.

The people who own real property are usually the ones who call the shots. They're often a shy lot, especially when something shady is going on. And, since property ownership can so often be equated with money and power, something shady is often going on. We ought to know who these people are.

The techniques for following the property trail can be used to uncover slumlords or to find out who is putting up the house on the corner lot. But, again, the information is public and yours by right.

As before, I'm going to give you an assignment and then walk you through a hypothetical case. This assignment could be easier or more difficult, depending on your unique circumstances.

Assignment: **AT RANDOM, PICK A BUILDING IN THE NEAREST DOWNTOWN AREA AND FIND OUT WHO OWNS IT.**

If you are very energetic, you could then use the techniques covered earlier in this chapter and find out everything you can about the person, or persons, who own the property.

Here we go. We pick the quaint, four-story office building that houses our favorite bookstore. Its address is 5561 Dogbone Avenue.

Each state and city has its own method for collecting and recording property information. Fortunately, there's always a general resemblance among the systems. The names of individual agencies may differ, but the concept is the same. If you are uncertain what the agency in your community is called, contact city hall and describe the kind of information you want. They'll tell you the name of the proper agency to approach.

Our first stop is the city tax assessor's office. There we examine a series of maps showing each building in the city. From the map we obtain a reference number that corresponds with a logbook containing the property information for that map section. (In many tax assessor offices, this process will be done by a clerk at your request.) The logbook tells us that the taxes for the property at 5561 Dogbone Avenue were paid by Amalgamated Management Systems Inc. An address is listed for AMS Inc. We also learn the value at which the property is assessed.

We check the name Amalgamated Management Systems Inc. in the telephone directory, but find no listing for it. A call to directory assistance is equally fruitless.

At the address listed by the tax assessor for AMS Inc. we find an office building. The name on the door, however, is not Amalgamated Management Systems Inc., but Windom Enterprises.

Our next stop is the corporate division of the Secretary of State (not the U.S. Secretary of State—each state has its own Secretary or a similar office). There we ask to examine the articles of incorporation for Amalgamated Management Systems. From this document we discover the names of the AMS Inc. board of directors—Eliot Goodwin, Esther Madison, and Douglas Windom, a familiar name.

A similar search of the records for Windom Enterprises determines that Douglas Windom is the company president. It also reveals that Esther Madison is on the board of directors, along with two others, of this company also.

We next stop by the county courthouse to check with the clerk of court regarding any criminal or civil litigation involving Amalgamated Management Systems Inc., Windom Enterprises, or any of the people we know to be associated with those companies. There's nothing.

While at the courthouse we visit the county recorder. This is the office, if you recall, where all property transactions are recorded. There we search the yearly general index for the names of any of the individuals or companies.

Are we finished? Not even close. Any mention of any of the target names provides us with more to research. In addition, we know nothing about the relationship among the people who operate the companies. Each coveted piece of information leads us a little closer. Closer to what? I don't know. Maybe nothing. That's why we're investigating. To find out.

As you can see, the property trail can be difficult to follow. Most property trails are a lot less convoluted than the one I've presented here. But the level of complexity increases as the value of the property under investigation increases. The more powerful the people involved, the better they are at masking their business interests. Often—not always, but often—they mask their interests not just for the sake of privacy, but because they're hiding something. And that knowledge is the incentive for locking on, for persisting. Because whatever they're hiding is worth finding out.

These scenarios shouldn't be interpreted as the only way to get the job done. For each scenario, I ordered the steps in a fashion that seemed logical to me. You don't have to follow the same order, or even the same steps. This isn't like a recipe or the assembly instructions for a swing set. It's more like a scavenger hunt.

This is how detectives operate. We dig a little, make a few educated guesses, then dig a little more. And then, a little more.

Chapter 5

THE DETECTIVE AS ARCHAEOLOGIST

I tried to trust. I never read my lover's journal. I wouldn't watch his window, look in his address book, follow him. I saved those spy tactics for my professional life.

But when I was in his kitchen, I couldn't help myself. I studied the trash. Can he really be using sculpting gel, or has another woman made herself at home? Has he been using pantyhose for a thousand helpful household uses, or for burglaries? Have I ever seen him peel an apple? I let it go.

And then it was a sunny weekend afternoon in late fall, and in a burst of ecological goodwill we took all the Sunday papers from all year to be recycled. I noticed an unfamiliar hand had worked the crosswords. An hour of good detective work saved me a lifetime of cross-examination. Learn to look at what's left behind.

R.G.

Every time I turn the television to an educational channel, I see people patiently scraping away the surface of some equatorial desert, looking for evidence of our distant ancestors. They're looking for bits of bone, worn-out tools, broken pottery, the refuse of ancient cultures. In other words, they're looking for trash.

Archaeologists are detectives. They do what detectives do—pay attention to small details, think about them, note patterns, then piece the puzzle together into a logical form. It's effective whether your subject is a two-million-year-old *Australopithecus africanus* or a thirty-six-year-old accountant. An archaeologist examining a fragment of a stone tool can speculate on the lives led by the people who made the tool. A detective examining discarded charge card receipts can speculate on the life led by the person who made the purchases.

We've been told that we are what we eat. We're also what we throw away. Our trash reveals a great deal about us, the sort of people we are, the sort of lives we lead. It's a valuable, if distasteful, source of information for the detective. A peek into a person's trash is a peek into their lives.

Legally, trash is fair game. The U.S. Supreme Court has said, in effect, if it's in the trash, you have no expectation of privacy. But be careful. State law is sometimes in conflict with federal law, so check the law in your state prior to snatching trash. You do not want to chance being a test case for your state.

In any event, you *cannot* trespass on private property to snatch trash. Trespassing is a crime. DON'T DO IT! Fortunately, most cities require trash be put at curbside for collection. Many cities also require trash to be placed in plastic bags, another boon for the detective. Nothing is worse than a soggy paper bag of garbage splitting open in your car.

To waste management professionals (there really are such people) there are two types of refuse: trash and garbage. Most of us use the terms indiscriminately, but you should be aware of the difference. Garbage consists of the remains of food—corn cobs and pork chop scraps. Everything else is trash—broken bottles, old toys, newspapers, cardboard containers, and so on.

Detectives also divide refuse into two categories:

- Personal refuse—those items discarded at homes and apartments. It consists of both trash and garbage.

- Business refuse—those items discarded at offices and places of employment. It is mainly trash, primarily paper.

Trash is much easier to snatch in residential areas than in cities. To snatch trash from specific apartments or offices in buildings, you must rely on others, a prospect no detective relishes. The more people involved, the more likely something will go wrong.

To snatch trash from apartment and office buildings, you need the cooperation of the building superintendent or the cleaning staff. That usually means a bribe. For a small fee, either the super or a janitor might be willing to set aside the trash desired.

If a bribe offends you, or seems too risky, or you're on a limited budget, think about taking a job with the cleaning service. The problem with that tactic is that it requires time to arrange and, if the cleaning service is a large one, there is no guarantee you'll be assigned to the building in question.

The Operation

Before we discuss what sort of information you can expect to cull from your subject's trash, let's consider these steps in the operation of acquiring it:

- Pre-snatch logistics
- The snatch
- Tools
- Examination site

Please, try to control the urge to crack jokes about investigating being a dirty business.

Pre-snatch Logistics

After you've reached the decision to lift somebody's trash, give some thought to how you're actually going to do it. This may not be the raid at Entebbe, but a little forethought can save a lot of aggravation.

Find out when the trash is collected. The easiest way is to call city hall. That's why they're there. They'll be able to tell you if the trash is collected by a public or private service. They'll also be able to give you the telephone number of the collectors. Tell them you're house-sitting for a few weeks and want to know the trash collection schedule. Be sure to find out both the day and approximate time of collection.

Drive by the subject's house late the night before the trash is collected, or very early in the morning—3:00 A.M. is a good hour. Some people put their trash out at night to save them from having to get up early in the morning. If it's there, take it. People tend to be less active and less aware during the early-morning hours. Never waste an opportunity.

If you're going to make the snatch when it is dark, be sure to turn off the dome light inside your car. You don't want to illuminate yourself when you open the car door. And wear dark clothes. But don't get carried away and *don't* cork your face or use camouflage make-up. How would you explain it if you got stopped by the police for having a burned-out headlamp?

Consider how you're going to transport the trash to the examination site. You may want to line the trunk of your car with plastic. There are some disgusting things in the garbage and you don't want them to dirty your car.

Don't eat a large breakfast beforehand. And don't plan on eating for a while after. Unless you have a high tolerance for foul odors, and a cast iron stomach.

The Snatch

Regardless of your preparation, when you actually step out of your vehicle to make the snatch you're going to feel conspicuous. You're going to feel like you're on center court at Wimbledon, as if everybody is watching.

Despite that feeling, it's highly unlikely anybody is going to notice. People tend to put their trash at the curb and then forget about it. How often do you see *your* garbagemen?

Obviously, the snatch should be done discreetly. Leave the car door open after you get out; it's quicker and quieter. Act as if taking trash from the curb and stuffing it into your rear seat or trunk is a normal routine. Don't rush, don't cast guilty glances at the houses, don't drop anything. Just walk quickly but calmly, pick up the trash, put it into the car, and leave. It's that simple.

What should you do if you're spotted? Or worse, confronted? I don't know. It's never happened to me. There are no hard and fast rules for situations like that. You have to play it by ear.

I *can* give you some advice. If you're spotted, ignore it. Act as if the person wasn't there, even if that person is your subject. If you are confronted, I advise lying. Tell the person you're a researcher for the Department of Health and are doing spot checks to determine what sort of trash is being discarded.

Will it work? Who knows? Detective work is like the best jazz—it demands the ability to improvise, to think quickly and fluidly, to adapt to the unexpected. Do what you think will work.

Take along a partner, if possible. It makes the snatch quicker and you're less likely to be confronted if you're caught.

Tools

It's important to have the proper equipment when doing a trash search. It just makes everything easier. Here's what you'll need:

- *Several pairs of plastic or rubber gloves.* There's usually a lot of nasty stuff in personal trash, things you don't want to touch. You should also be careful not to cut yourself on used razors and open tin cans. Business trash is usually much less messy.

- *Something to dull the stench.* That is, if you must do the actual search inside. Aerosol sprays are good, and a bandanna scented with something is invaluable when tied around your face.

- *A probing tool.* A stick or pencil will do, anything to poke through the chicken bones and sodden broccoli.

- *Fresh trash bags.* You'll have to re-bag the

stuff and throw it away again. Extra plastic trash bags are essential if the garbage you collected was in a paper bag.

- *A camera.* This is vital if you need documentation for any reason, a child-custody case for example.

Examination Site

Garbage stinks. If possible, find a well-ventilated area for the examination. A field, a garage, any place with a lot of space. Don't use your home or office unless you live or work by yourself. Or *want* to live or work by yourself.

The Information

The actual process of sifting through refuse can be tedious and often repulsive. Fortunately for the detective, although not for the environment, most personal trash is packaging—the boxes and bags things are sold in. If you're not interested in the quality or quantity of the items purchased, most packaging can be shoved to one side.

As a general rule, unless you're looking for a specific item—a telephone bill, for example—you must examine everything. Pay attention. Nothing should be overlooked.

This is especially true of business trash. You must look at each piece of paper that's thrown away. Not just the letters, the invoices, and the receipts. Each piece of paper. People write notes on Post-its, on envelopes, on scrap paper, on napkins. A scribbled telephone number on a scrap of yellow paper might be of vital importance. Pay attention. Pay close attention.

What can a person's trash tell you? More than they'd want you to know. You can gather a lot of information about your subject's—

- Friends and family
- Finances
- Drinking or drug habits
- Diet
- Sexual behavior
- Physical and emotional condition

Trash talks.

Friends and Family

Not everybody saves letters and cards. Return addresses on envelopes can be important, and the contents of the letters can be very revealing. A few days after holidays and birthdays are good times to check for addresses.

Discarded telephone bills can provide you with the telephone numbers of your subject's long-distance friends and associates. If the subscriber can give his account number (which is listed on the bill) and the specific page of the bill where the number is noted, telephone companies will give out the name of the person who is listed for each number called. I'm not suggesting you lie to the telephone company; I'm merely passing on the information.

Finances

Look for discarded charge card slips, overdue or late bills, letters from collection agencies. A lot of people throw away their paycheck stubs. Automatic teller receipts are always dated and often include a notation of the owner's current checking balance. Check for crumpled up lottery tickets. Look inside every discarded bag—when people purchase things they often throw away the receipt with the bag.

A thorough search through the garbage can tell you how and where a person spends his money.

Drinking or Drug Habits

Your subject's drinking habits can sometimes be determined from the trash. Count the bottles. They'll tell you not only how much he drinks, but how much he spends on alcohol. In addition, it is sometimes helpful to know your subject's drinking preferences, so pay attention to brand labels.

Hangover remedies can be enlightening. Look for the ends of celery stained with tomato juice (Bloody Marys), or empty Gatorade bottles (fluid replacement for alcohol dehydration). Gatorade, don't forget, is also used by athletes, so it is significant only when in conjunction with other signs of heavy drinking.

Look for matchbooks to discover if the subject hangs out in bars. Always check the inside covers for telephone numbers and addresses.

The use of illegal drugs is more difficult to detect. Examine discarded plastic bags for marijuana seeds and stems. Note any small brown vials, which are popular cocaine and crack containers. Look for triangular scraps of paper that might have been used as cocaine bindles. Corners of magazine pages are popular bindles; they hold a crease well, have a smooth surface, and lie flat in the pocket.

Diet

Diet sometimes becomes an issue in child-custody cases. The trash can show the sort of meals the child eats at home. Simply noting the garbage can help determine if the child exists on a diet of Spaghettios and frozen dinners or home-cooked meals with fresh fruits and vegetables. Many grocery stores now have computers that itemize groceries by brand name and price on the receipt. You can often find grocery receipts inside discarded grocery bags. Courts are often interested in how much junk food a child eats.

Sexual Behavior

Investigating a person's sexual behavior is distasteful, but sometimes it's important. And even if you aren't specifically interested in your subject's sexual habits, a detective can never have too much information. Knowing your subject's menstrual cycle might somehow come in handy. For the most part, though, whatever sexual detritus you find in the trash just confirms what you already suspect.

Contraceptive methods can be determined from empty tubes of spermicidal foam, foil condom packages, discarded containers of birth control pills.

Check wadded tissues for used condoms. In a man's trash, empty tubes of K-Y or petroleum jelly might indicate homosexual activity, as could a lot of laxative packages. Look for bottles that contained scented or flavored oils.

Special interests can sometimes be determined from discarded magazines and newsletters. If alternative newspapers are found, check the personal sections for circled advertisements.

Again, pay attention, examine everything, and *think*. It never hearts to think.

Physical and Emotional Condition

Look for discarded pill containers and medicine bottles. Make note of over-the-counter medicine packages or bottles—antacids, analgesics, sleeping aids. They can tell you a lot about the subject's general health.

On prescription containers, note the name of the drug, the dosage, the number of pills issued, and the doctor's name. The *Physician's Desk Reference* at the public library can tell you what the drug is, and what medical problems it is used to treat.

If you're covering a person's trash over a period of time and notice a marked decrease in the amount of food being consumed, it could indicate emotional distress (it could also indicate a new diet—look for other signs of distress). A lot of damp tissues could mean that the subject has been crying a lot, or simply that the subject has a cold.

Evidence of every malady from chronic aches and

pains to full-blown psychotic episodes can be found in the trash.

To summarize, everything that gets thrown away tells something about the person who throws it away. Everything that gets cast aside has a message. All you have to do is make the effort to find it and understand it.

Chapter 6

HOW TO FIND JUST ABOUT ANYBODY

One of the first things lawyers learn is not to ask too many questions. When I'd send Greg out to find a witness or a missing client, I never asked how he did it. It was enough for me that he did.

Then one day I wanted to mail a letter to some friends, but I couldn't remember their address. I didn't have my address book with me, and I didn't want to go home to get it. Suddenly, I was helpless. I had no idea how to find my own friends.

So I did the smart thing. I asked a detective.

Greg made a few suggestions and handed me the telephone receiver. Five minutes later, I had the envelope addressed.

Since that time, I've been able to discover the address of the man who put the dent in my fender. And the address of a city council member who was avoiding a subpoena. And the address of the guy at the gym.

This stuff comes in handy.

R.G.

People today seem to come and go like tumble-weeds. Rootless, they drift along, attracting little attention and leaving few signs they were ever there. Close friends move across town and disappear out of our lives. Family members lose touch with each other with alarming ease. Lovers argue, separate, and fade away.

Where do they all go? How can you find them? How do you find a witness to an accident, for example, or to a crime? Or a person who owes you money? If friends and family are so difficult to keep track of, how can anybody hope to find a near stranger?

In this chapter you'll learn how to track people down. You'll be given some general guidelines on the techniques for locating people, and, through the use of scenarios, you'll be shown how to put those guidelines to use.

Finding people combines the best and the worst aspects of detective work. Sometimes it's tedious and monotonous, requiring hours of dreary footwork. At other times it demands creativity and elaborate cleverness.

A few years ago I was asked to find a certain doctor. He'd been present while the police interrogated a man suspected of an attempted murder. There was some question about the voluntariness of the man's statement to the police. The doctor, I was told, might be able to shed some light on the matter.

The only information I was given was the doctor's surname, a common one—Smith—and that he'd worked in the emergency room of a certain small-town hospital on a certain night six weeks before. The town was near the border of two states and the hospital served communities in both.

It didn't seem like a tough assignment. I had nurtured a good relationship with one of the nursing supervisors at that hospital, so I called her. She was able to check the emergency room schedule and tell me the doctor's full name—Kevin Smith. Unfortunately, Dr. Smith wasn't on the ER schedule for the next two weeks.

The nursing supervisor also told me that the hospital often hired doctors from other areas to cover the ER on week nights. Those temporary doctors sometimes worked only one night every two weeks. Dr. Smith was apparently one of those doctors. She didn't have access to the personnel records, so she couldn't give me any more information.

I called the ER and said I needed to talk to Kevin Smith. I asked for him by name, as if I knew him, and I used that curt tone of voice used by doctors who are accustomed to being obeyed. The nurse told me what I already knew, that Dr. Smith wasn't there. I told her I'd call him at his office. As if an afterthought, I asked her if she had Kevin's other work number handy. She did. And she gave it to me without asking any questions. The area code was for the other state.

I called the number, and learned it was for an internal medicine clinic in a town about thirty miles from the border. When I asked for Dr. Kevin Smith, I was told he no longer worked there. He had resigned a month earlier. The receptionist said she had no idea where he was currently employed. She didn't know whether he still lived in the area. No, she wouldn't give me his former address or telephone number. She was sorry she couldn't help, but rules are rules, and they were very busy, thank you for calling, good-bye.

I'd run into a dead end, but I wasn't too discouraged. I was a detective, after all, and I had all the detective's tools at my disposal. Which included telephone books for that area. In the yellow pages, under "Physician," Dr. Kevin Smith was listed. Unfortunately, the only listing was the clinic's number, the one I had just called. There was no listing for Kevin Smith in the white pages.

I called directory assistance for the communities surrounding the town where the clinic was located and found four Kevin Smiths. I called each of them, but none was a doctor.

I called all the internal medicine clinics in that area. No Kevin Smith.

I went to the public library and looked up Kevin Smith in the *American Medical Directory*. That gave me the name of the school he attended and the year he graduated, as well as the name of the clinic where he had been employed. By looking through a few other listings for the same area I found the names of two other doctors who had attended the same medical school at the same time as Dr. Smith.

I also checked the city directory for the community in which the clinic was located. Nothing.

Back at my office I began to work the telephone. I called the medical school, giving one of the other doctor's names, and saying I was trying to find my old buddy Kevin. The secretary at the alumni center had an address for him, and kindly supplied it to me. It was the address of the clinic where Smith no longer worked.

I called both the doctors, saying I was from the alumni center and looking for Dr. Smith. Neither of them had seen him since graduating from medical school.

I called the nearest chapter of the American Medical Association; they only had the clinic address. I called half a dozen medical journals to see if they'd received a change of address. Dr. Smith subscribed to only one of the journals, and it was delivered to the clinic.

I called fitness clubs in the area of the clinic to see if Kevin Smith was a member; I called golf courses; I called racquet clubs. Nothing, nothing, nothing.

I was definitely getting discouraged. But I was a detective, after all, with all the detective's tools at my disposal. I drank a beer and threw darts for forty-five minutes. Everybody has his own method for clearing his mind.

Finally, I got an idea. I called the clinic again. This time I identified myself as a representative of a well-known computer company. I said we'd received a number of complaints about keyboards from customers who had purchased a certain model of computer and we'd been authorized by the company to replace those keyboards free of charge. I said I had Dr. Smith's new keyboard and asked when he wanted it delivered.

I have no idea if Dr. Smith even owned a personal computer. But I thought it was the sort of expensive, high-tech contraption a doctor might own and I surmised the receptionist would be equally ignorant. It didn't seem likely, though, that she'd refuse to cooperate with a person offering a free replacement part for a complex and expensive piece of electronic equipment.

I didn't ask to speak with Dr. Smith, and I didn't give the receptionist a chance to tell me he wasn't there. I just gave my little rap and asked when the keyboard should be delivered.

The receptionist explained that Dr. Smith no longer worked there and she didn't know where he'd gone. I said the offer was only good for a limited time. She hesitated, then put me on hold. A short time later another doctor got on the line, a friend of Dr. Smith. Smith, I learned, hadn't moved; he'd simply joined the staff of a health maintenance organization. The doctor gave me Kevin Smith's new work address and telephone number as well as his home address and his unlisted home telephone number.

Piece of cake.

Given time, almost anybody can be tracked down. For the most part, the people that detectives find aren't actively hiding. They just aren't where they were expected to be. They've switched jobs, moved, married, gone on vacation, joined a religious order. They've changed their lives in some way.

That change doesn't have to be drastic. Even a

minor change, over time, can have long-reaching effects. Physicists have a phrase for similar phenomena—sensitive dependence on initial conditions. A small event can cause unpredictable and radical alterations. And the longer the period of time from the event, the more radical the alterations. A neighbor moves fifteen blocks away—he has a new set of neighbors, shops at new markets, fills his prescriptions at a new pharmacy. It's inconvenient to see his old friends. People ask each other, "Whatever happened to old what's-his-name?" After twelve months, it's as if he'd never lived in the old neighborhood.

How can you find "old what's-his-name"? First, assume that the project is going to take considerable time. It might not, but it's best to approach it as if it will. That gives you the proper pace. Endurance, attitude, and attention to detail should bring you through. In addition, tracking people will be a lot easier if you keep in mind a few basic tenets:

1. *Nobody lives in a vacuum.* People are interdependent. Most of us are connected to others in some fashion—through friendship, family ties, neighbors, co-workers. The more people you interact with, the easier it is to find you.

2. *People are creatures of habit.* It's easier to change your address, your career, or even your appearance than it is to break a habit. Habits can be anything from the brand of cigarette one smokes or the games one plays to the manner in which one dresses.

The more habits you have, the easier it is to find you.

3. *People are reluctant to change affiliations.* Democrats tend to remain Democrats, Methodists usually stick with a Methodist church, Red Sox fans will *always* have broken hearts every fall. The stronger and more numerous your affiliations, the easier it is to find you.

4. *Few people are free from bureaucracy.* While it's true that an appalling number of people are homeless or live day to day by panhandling, most people still have utility bills. They still drive cars and pay rent and have debts. The more bureaucratic ties you have, the easier it is to find you.

Unless people are *actively* making an effort to disappear, they leave a trail. All you have to do is follow it.

Every attempt to find somebody starts with what is called a guide. A guide is a solid piece of information the detective can seize hold of and work with. It can be a name, an address, a telephone number, any link with the subject. The guide will lead you in a certain direction. As you follow, you'll gather more information, more guides. It's a cumulative process, and eventually one of those guides will lead you to the person you seek.

We'll examine three hypothetical scenarios to demonstrate how the process works. In each scenario we'll begin with a different guide and follow it to the end.

Keep in mind that these scenarios are models. They aren't road maps for tracking people down. Rather, they're meant to be used as a compass, a tool to help you get your bearings. While reading them, try to think of other ways to get the same result. The result, when you get down to it, is what really counts. Finding the person you're after. There aren't any wrong paths—just different ways of getting there.

Scenario 1

We are asked to find a woman named Deborah Halperin. The only information we have is her name and a two-year-old address.

Obviously, our first move is to go to that address. She might still live there, after all. Not everybody moves like tinkers.

The address is an old house, partitioned into four apartment units. Unfortunately, Ms. Halperin doesn't live in any of them. (You didn't actually think she was going to be there, did you? What sort of exercise would that be?) We ask the neighbors, all of whom have lived in the building for nearly a year. None is familiar with the name Halperin. We do, however, obtain the name and address of the landlord.

Before bothering the landlord, we stop at the post office to do an address search. Anybody with a dollar and a lot of patience can request an address search. The post office is required to provide you with a person's forwarding address. It's public information. The post office, however, is only required to keep forwarding addresses for one year. Fortunately, postal employees are as slow to do their paperwork as the rest of us. You can sometimes obtain a forwarding address that's over a year old.

Not in this case, however. The post office has been sadly efficient. We waste a buck and learn nothing about Ms. Halperin.

The landlord, fortunately, has been less conscientious about his paperwork. He still has Deborah Halperin's rental application on file. Landlords are a cautious group of people and they ask a lot of personal questions on their applications, including such diverse questions as the applicant's place of employment, next of kin, and prior residence. Any such information can be a useful guide.

Rental applications *are not* public documents. The landlord is under no obligation to show it to us. However, it's been my experience that landlords can usually be persuaded to help. How that's done is a matter of discretion. I suggest you tell the truth, if you think it'll work. A monetary contribution might also be effective (see Chapter 4 re: bribes).

For whatever reason (whether out of the kindness of his heart or because we've made his pockets a little heavier), the landlord lets us examine the rental application. We learn that when she moved into the apartment, Deborah Halperin was employed by Big Rudy's Seafood Restaurant. We also get the name, address, and telephone number of her mother (as next of kin).

The mother is the obvious choice. Mothers almost always know where their children are. The difficulty is in deciding on the proper approach. While mothers usually know where their children are, they're also protective; they'll want to know why *you* want to know where their children are. Do we go to the mother, knock on the door, and tell her who we are and what we want? Or do we call her on the telephone and run a scam on her, tell her we're an old friend of her daughter? Or some combination of the two approaches?

Usually, the choice of approach is related to the reasons you're looking for a person. Obviously, if you don't want the subject to know why you're looking for her (or even that you *are* looking for her), you make an oblique approach. For the purposes of this scenario, we'll assume our purposes are benign. We have nothing to hide. We go straight to the mother's house and pound manfully on the door.

Mom sees our cheerful, smiling face and gladly tells us her daughter Deborah is now living at the Wiltshire Apartments. Nothing to it.

But what if Mom *hadn't* liked our cheerful, smiling face? What if she tossed us out on our ear? Are we out of luck?

Not at all. We can examine Mom's trash looking for signs of Deborah. We can conduct a surveillance of the house and tail every young woman who visits. We can wait a week and try some variation of the original plan of calling and scamming Mom.

And if that doesn't work? We still have the restaurant mentioned on the rental application. If she no longer works there, we can check with her former co-workers. If they don't know where she currently lives, they might know the names of other friends who might know.

And if that doesn't work? We can follow the paper trail on Deborah Halperin. Does she have a car registered? Is she registered to vote? We can call the utility companies and see if Deborah Halperin is a customer.

And if *that* doesn't work? We'll think of something else.

Scenario 2

Our client has seen his wife getting out of a blue sedan with license number P344002 at two o'clock on the preceding Friday afternoon. We are asked to identify and find the person who was driving the car.

Our only guide is the license number. Most detectives who've been in the business for a while have developed contacts that will run a check on license numbers. As a novice, this is a luxury you probably don't have. So our obvious first step is to check with the Department of Motor Vehicles.

Each state and local DMV has its own rules regarding the distribution of information. Very few state agencies will provide you with the information over the telephone. Given the least opportunity, bureaucrats usually revert to type—they become petty, mean-spirited, and small-minded. They'll demand a written request detailing why you want the information. I suggest you approach the city motor vehicle registration office. These folks are usually more cooperative and more professional than their state counterparts, but even they can be difficult.

The police, of course, have almost instant access to motor vehicle information. However, there's little point in consulting the police, even if you have a legit-

imate reason for wanting the information. They're
not in the business of tracing a vehicle unless a crime
is involved. And if a crime is involved, they're not
likely to share the information with you.

The DMV, then, is your best bet. Your approach to
the DMV will reflect your own personal style. I'll tell
you the approach I use for those times I haven't been
able to get a license check. You're welcome to use it,
if it meets your standards.

I lie. (Yes, I realize that lying is not acceptable
behavior in polite society. But polite society rarely
needs to track people down. Do you want the information or not? You can rejoin polite society later.) I
telephone the local DMV and lie to a clerk. The lie
usually goes something like this:

> *I'm just traveling through town and I
> stopped at a drug store for some aspirin. As I
> was getting out of my car, I saw this woman
> put a package on top of her car while she
> unlocked it. Then she got into the car and
> drove off, with the package still on top. It fell
> off as she was pulling out of the parking lot. It
> looks like a birthday present for a child. I tried
> to stop her but she didn't hear me. But I got her
> license number. It's P344002 or 03. Can you tell
> me who owns the car?*

These are the bare bones, of course. But it gives
you the idea. It shows you're a concerned and considerate person for wanting to return a lost birthday
present; it demonstrates a sense of urgency since
you're just traveling through town; it gives the clerk
every reason in the world to want to help you.

Of course, it doesn't have to be a woman who lost a birthday present. It could have been a student who lost a knapsack full of books, or an old man who dropped his bifocal sunglasses.

It's a good, functional, generic lie. And we use it. And it works. We find that license number P344002 is registered as a blue 1986 Chevrolet belonging to Robert Jeffrey Delaney of 2323 Worsted Road.

Now we have to ask ourselves the important question. Is he our man? Was he driving his car last Friday at two o'clock in the afternoon?

Who knows? Delaney has to be interviewed (interviewing skills are discussed in a separate chapter). If he denies driving the car, then he should be able to provide us with other leads to follow. And as long as we have something to guide us, we're in business.

Scenario 3

We're asked to find a man called Twist. The only information we have about Twist is that a couple of years ago he was known to hang out at a bar called the Madison Grill.

We check the telephone directory, but find no listing for the Madison Grill, nor is directory assistance helpful. We call the local police dispatcher. Police and fire department dispatch operators commonly have detailed maps and charts showing the location of every building in their precinct. The reason we called the police dispatcher rather than the fire department is because police officers are more familiar with bars. Bars are often the scene of trouble.

The police dispatcher tells us the Madison Grill closed over a year ago, but gives us its old address. We go there and find a boarded up shell of a building that had obviously once housed a saloon for serious drinkers.

Out next stop is the Alcohol Control Board. Although the name may vary, every state has an agency that regulates and enforces the liquor licensing laws. The agency keeps records of the licenses issued.

We ask for the name and address of the owner who was issued a license for the Madison Grill. You may hear the expression "DBA" used when talking with an employee of the Alcohol Control Board. DBA is an acronym for "doing business as." It's the name under which a business operates. In this particular case, the Madison Grill is the DBA.

We learn that the liquor license for the Madison Grill was issued to John McCormick. The license had lapsed. We also learn McCormick's address.

From here on, it's grunt work. Knocking on doors and asking questions. McCormick may not know Twist, or may not know his real name, or may no know where he can be found. But he'll have the names of Madison Grill employees, and they might know. Or they'll know the names of some of the bar's regulars, and they might know. One way or another, Twist will be found.

And that's how it works. You get one scrap of information and you grab it, work it until it reveals other scraps of information. Once the search for a person begins, it is more common to have too much information than too little. The difficulty is in knowing which scraps of information are likely to pay off.

As I said earlier, given enough time, almost anybody can be tracked down. All it takes is a little creativity, a little planning, a little attention, and a whole lot of persistence.

Chapter 7

VERBAL SEDUCTION

In the course of our investigations Greg went down many mean streets and into mean bars. He talked to violent men and women who believed in their right to bear arms and use them if riled. He spent hours alone with rapists and killers. Some were men behind bars who had nothing to lose. He went unarmed, and he returned unscathed. That's because people can be verbally seduced, if you know how.

Only one time did Greg come back with blood on his hands. He had, in self-defense, punched a Rottweiler in the teeth. A Rottweiler is a dog—a cross between a Doberman and a Jeep.

R.G.

Al Capone said you can get further with a kind word and a gun than with a kind word alone. Big Al never would have made it as a detective. No subtlety.

And subtlety is what it takes to get information from a person who doesn't want to give it to you.

I had to interview a young woman whose husband had been badly injured in a fight. My information was that the fight took place as a result of a bad drug deal. Although I doubted that the woman would want to talk to me (I was working for the man accused of putting her husband in the hospital), I felt I had to try to speak with her. She might know something about the events preceding the fight.

I went to her home and she invited me in. As I walked in, I noticed a bunch of educational toys for an infant. On a coffee table a group of photographs were lying on the envelope they had come in, as if she'd put them down to answer the door. A pair of books on parenting were also in the room. Obviously, this was the adoring mother of a first child.

I explained who I was, who I worked for, and why I was there. The woman frowned, obviously not happy to see me. As I was explaining, the child waddled into the room. She was about two years old and dressed in an expensive sleeper, one, I would have guessed, that was out of their price range.

Like all very young children, she didn't know to avoid strangers. She walked straight up to me and demanded "Up." So I picked her up and told her what a pretty little girl she was. For a few moments I ignored the mother and spoke to the child. I sat on a hassock and gave her everything in my pockets that I thought might entertain her.

Once the child was happily playing with my car keys, I looked up and smiled at her mother. She was smiling back. I told her again who I was and why I needed to speak with her. I did *not* tell her how wonderful her daughter was. That could backfire; she might think I only wanted to butter her up. Which for the most part, was true. Instead, I let her *see* that I liked the child.

The woman sat down and answered my questions, while I continued to entertain and tickle her daughter. I interrupted her once or twice to make a face and a silly noise at the child. Then I asked Mom to repeat what she had said, which she did happily.

After all, how could she refuse somebody who so obviously appreciated what an exceptional child she had?

Subtlety.

When conducting an interview, a good detective engages in a form of seduction—verbal seduction. He creates a mood designed to elicit the information he wants. He invites the subject to like him and trust him. He allows the subject to realize how singular and unique he or she is. And he provides the subject with an opportunity to speak and be heard. Verbal seduction is a total engagement of mind and body, the detective's and the subject's.

Verbal seduction, at its best, should appear spontaneous. And there *should* always be an element of spontaneity in an interview. But that spontaneity needs to be laid on a solid foundation of basic skills. In order to consistently get good interviews the detective needs—

- Good interpersonal skills
- Pre-interview preparation
- A way to get in the subject's door
- Familiarity with standard interviewing technique
- An understanding of body language

Of course, you *can* get a good interview while being absolutely ignorant of these things. But you can't do it consistently. And consistency is what pays the bills.

Interpersonal Skills

The personal qualities required to be a good interviewer are these:

- Good manners
- Flexibility

- An intuitive understanding of human nature
- Self-confidence

These skills are critical. We'll examine them all.

Good Manners

I realize that manners might seem an unlikely qualification for a detective. But don't confuse manners with the social graces. Having good manners involves more than not chewing with your mouth open. The essence of good manners is putting other people at ease, making them feel comfortable, putting their wants before your own. A person who insists on the unconditional use of social graces may be well trained, but is not well mannered.

I want to stress the importance of putting people at their ease. People are usually more willing to give you information if they feel comfortable. Mata Hari, after all, didn't become a famous spy because of her ability as an interviewer. I'm not suggesting you sleep with a witness (a quick word of advice about sleeping with witnesses—*don't*), but I am suggesting you make every reasonable (and perhaps even an unreasonable) effort to make your witness comfortable.

I had to interview a young couple who had witnessed an attempted murder. The couple and their two small children lived in a small, fetid mobile home that reeked of stale sweat, garbage, and dirty diapers. I'd come unannounced and they were embarrassed at the slovenly condition of the trailer. Despite their embarrassment, they invited me in, asked me to sit, and offered me a cup of coffee. I didn't want to go in (the summer heat made the stench nearly unbearable), I didn't want to sit (the chair was filthy), and I didn't want any coffee (I hate coffee). But good manners (and the job) required it. I went in, sat down, leaned back in the chair, and said I'd love a cup of coffee.

The husband had been working on a carburetor when I arrived. His hands were too greasy to touch the child so I held the baby while the wife poured the coffee. The child was wearing nothing but a cloth diaper that was saturated with feces.

I sipped the coffee and we chatted for a while about the heat and the difficulty of keeping a house clean with two children. As they relaxed I slowly led the conversation into the crime they'd witnessed. By the time I was ready to leave, they were calling me by my first name.

When I got back to the office my clothes smelled of dirty diapers. My co-workers held their noses and avoided me. I had to go home and change clothes. That, too, was good manners.

Putting people at ease is usually critical for conducting a good interview. There *is* a time and place for rudeness, but we'll cover that later.

Flexibility.

It's difficult to predict how a total stranger will behave. Each moment of an interview reveals something about the person being interviewed, what upsets or angers him, what he finds important or interesting. During an interview a good detective will constantly re-evaluate his view of the subject, and then act on the new evaluation. You must be able to rapidly adjust to that changing perspective. A good detective is something of a social contortionist—he bends and shapes himself to match the subject.

An Understanding of Human Nature.

You can't put people at ease if you don't know what makes them comfortable. Fortunately, most of us have a fairly good intuitive feel for human nature. Unfortunately, we rarely put it to use.

We know people want to be believed. We know they want to be respected, to be genuinely understood and appreciated. A good detective, rather than spend all his time probing for information, will focus at least part of his concentration on understanding his subject. This is especially important at the beginning of the interview.

In most circumstances, your intuitive understanding of human nature, plus a little consideration, will give you enough insight into your subject to enable you to get the information you need.

Self-confidence.

Quiet self-confidence is a critical component of the detective's temperament. You have to believe in your ability to cope with any situation that arises. Don't confuse self-confidence with cockiness or a lack of caution. A cocky detective is a stupid detective, and stupid detectives don't stay in business.

Self-confidence communicates itself to witnesses.

I always try to behave as if the person I want to talk to also wants to talk to me. It's rarely true, but if I *act* as if it's so, sometimes people *think* it's so. And then they answer my questions.

Pre-interview Preparation

Marathon runners don't run without stretching first. Concert pianists don't perform without warming up first. Even Mike Tyson doesn't box without training first. So it should be no surprise that a good detective doesn't do an interview without preparing first.

The primary reason for preparation is to gain a degree of familiarity with the case. The more comfortable you are with the facts, the more comfortable you'll be during the interview. Give some thought to these suggestions.

Clarify to yourself your reasons for the interview.

Why do you need to talk to this person? What sort of information does he or she have? What sort of information are you looking for? This should seem obvious. But I once drove a couple hundred miles, found a missing witness, and did a great interview that seemed to set the stage for an insanity defense. It wasn't until I was back at the office that I realized the lawyer I was working for was trying to have some evidence suppressed on the basis that the arrest had been illegal. At that point he was more interested in information about the client's arrest than a defense for the trial. There wouldn't even *be* a trial if the evidence was suppressed. But I was so jazzed about the insanity issue that I'd forgotten to ask a single question about the arrest itself. I had to drive the two hundred miles all over again.

Review all material about the case.

The more familiar you are with the facts, the easier the interview will be. You never know what tiny bit of information will turn the case around—a description of a car, the name of a tavern, anything. A weapons dealer once decided that I could be trusted just because I referred to a certain man by his nickname. The nickname was all I knew about the man. It was enough.

Think of a general approach to the witness.

For example, you'll approach a friendly witness differently than you would a hostile one, or a bank officer differently than a gas-pump jockey. But keep the approach general and be prepared to alter it.

Don't over-prepare.

This relates to the point I just made. While you can't have too much information about the case, you can prep yourself into tunnel vision. When an interview isn't going the way you anticipated, dump that approach and try another. Be ready and willing to change tactics quickly.

Some people even write questions out in advance, a practice I feel makes interviews too mechanical and closes you off from other potentially important avenues of inquiry. It might be a good idea to note the main topics you want to cover, but be prepared to abandon them if something promising turns up. Don't be surprised when you have to discard all your plans and preparation. If the situation calls for it, don't hesitate.

Consider the place for the interview.

People will respond differently in different environments. Before the interview you need to decide on the best place to conduct it.

- *The subject's home.* This is the most common choice and, in my opinion, usually the best. As long as you take care that you're not seen as an invader, the subject will feel most at ease on his own territory. This can, of course, backfire. A very relaxed and confident subject could either resent your intrusion, or feel comfortable enough to lie to you more readily.

- *The subject's place of employment.* Very few people want to be interviewed by a detective where they work. They don't want their co-workers or employers to wonder about them. This option tends to elicit either of two extreme responses. The subject may refuse to talk with you (or simply give you a shallow, unsatisfactory inter-

view). Or he may tell you everything you
want to know without the usual song and
dance, just because he wants you to leave.

- *The detective's office.* This is good for more
  formal interviews. At the detective's office,
  the subject is more likely to tell you the
  things he thinks you ought to know. But he
  is likely to leave out what he may consider
  to be extraneous details, details that may,
  in fact, be of vital importance.

- *A neutral arena.* On occasion, it might be
  best to meet a subject at a restaurant or
  bar. I've done interviews in parks and
  beside swimming pools and in public libra-
  ries. A neutral arena is usually the best
  choice for a subject who is cooperative but
  wants to remain anonymous. The neighbor
  of a philandering husband, for example, or
  a witness in a personal-injury suit against
  the witness's employer.

Preparation can't guarantee a good interview any
more than a good interview can guarantee you'll get
good facts. But being properly prepared will certainly increase the chances of getting a good interview. And that's reason enough.

Getting in the Door

Why on earth would anybody willingly let a detective into his house? Unless the detective is working
for you, there is no way to know what he's up to. He

has his own agenda. To let such a person into your own home, to let him ask detailed, intimate questions, seems an act of madness. Yet, as I said earlier, most interviews take place at the home of the person being interviewed. Why *would* anybody let a detective into his home?

I'll tell you why. Because detectives make people *want* to let them in. Or make them think that they should, or must, let them in. They manufacture a reason for being let in, shape the reason to fit the situation and the individual, then sell it.

Here's how it's done:

- *Preparation.* I keep repeating this, I know. But it's so important. Before knocking on any door, the detective knows something about the person behind it. Even if he couldn't check out the person prior to the interview, he knows something. It might only be his knowledge of the neighborhood, or his impression of the house, or the toys scattered in the yard. It might only be his intuitive awareness of human behavior. But he knows *something* and he builds on that knowledge and uses it.

- *Pay attention to details.* Also repeated; also important. Seemingly minor details help you tailor your presentation to fit the situation and the person. Whenever you enter the home of a subject, give it a quick but thorough examination.

- *Smile.* It's harder to refuse a smiling face. There are, of course, times when it's inappropriate to display a smile. I was once unlucky enough to show up at the home of a witness about twenty minutes after the family had returned from the funeral of the man's wife. My eager, smiling face was totally out of place.

- *Stress your need.* The term *need* is more powerful than *want.* "I need to ask you a few questions." "I need a few minutes of your time."

- *Be ready to improvise.* You only have ten or fifteen seconds to evaluate the subject and decide whether to use, modify, or discard the approach you had tentatively decided on.

Once, on a drug case, I had to inspect the cellar of the client's apartment. According to the police reports, a quantity of drugs had been found in a locker in the cellar. The defense attorney needed to know who had access to the cellar.

Unfortunately, the client had moved out of the apartment after the arrest and it had been re-rented. I knew nothing about the new tenant—not the person's name, age, history, or even gender. But I knew the kinds of people who tended to live in that neighborhood, which was a fairly high crime area. I knew that the people who lived in the neighborhood were poor, that they were suspicious and resentful of authority, that they were familiar with hard times.

Armed with that basic knowledge, I knocked on the door. I had hoped that a man would answer. I figured it would be easier to talk a man into letting a total stranger snoop around the cellar. But an attractive young woman came to the door. The door opened into the kitchen, where a small black and white television was playing. The woman had apparently been reading *TV Guide,* because she held a copy in one hand with her finger marking her place. In the background, I could hear several children playing.

So, in the few seconds after the door was opened, my fund of information about the current occupant was dramatically increased. Very little of the information was directly helpful, but every bit of knowledge helps. It was unfortunate that the new tenant was a woman (women tend to be more cautious than men). To make matters worse, she was a very attractive young woman (it's been my experience that attractive women tend to be more suspicious). And there were children in the house (women with children are *very* protective). Since she was too young to be the mother of that many children, I assumed some were her own, some she was baby-sitting for working mothers. A young, attractive mother with a house full of children. It could only have been worse if she was pregnant. And confined to a wheel chair.

It was the television in the kitchen and the *TV Guide* in the woman's hand that I counted on. People who have a television in the kitchen watch a *lot* of television. And a lot of television shows are about police and detectives. And I was, after all, a detective. It was almost like an invitation.

I gave her a smile and introduced myself. As in all criminal cases, I identified myself. But instead of giving her a business card, which is my normal custom, I showed her my private detective license. Once she realized my reason for being there had nothing to do with her, that I only wanted to inspect her cellar, she asked me in.

The rest was easy. She asked me questions about the job, and I told her a few lies to make it sound more interesting. Then she gave me a guided tour of the cellar. The information I discovered down there, by the way, was instrumental in winning the case.

Although the key in this situation wasn't typical (being a detective hampers more often than it helps), it illustrates the need to pay attention to details and to use those details to improvise new tactics. The best approach to a man who answers the door in a T-shirt declaring, "They can take my gun when they pry it from my cold, dead fingers," will be different from that of a woman whose bookshelf contains the complete works of Andrea Dworkin.

Pay attention, pay attention, pay attention.

Basic Interviewing Technique

After all the forethought and planning, after you've managed to get in the door, you still have a lot of work to do. You still have to find out what that person knows.

There are no totally correct techniques for interviewing. Everybody has his own style, forged out of his own unique set of experiences. But these styles are usually based on the following standard interviewing practices:

1. Develop a rapport with the subject.

2. Ask the proper kind of question.

3. Maintain control of the interview.

These basic practices form the foundation on which individual styles are built. It's like any craft; once you master the basics the rest will come. Michelangelo probably started off sketching stick figures.

Develop a rapport with the subject.

Easy to say, but somewhat more difficult to do. Those details I keep advising you to pay attention to will give you clues to help you develop rapport. For example, if a man has the head of a moose over his mantel, choke back any animal-rights sentiments you may have and compliment him on the trophy. Ask him about the type of weapon and ammunition he used. Admire his skill at stalking the beast, even if you know that a moose is only slightly more wily than a Guernsey cow. You're there for information, not to proselytize.

Ask the proper kinds of questions.

At the beginning of an interview it is usually best to ask general questions (such as "What happened?"), then let the subject answer at his own pace and in his own words. Once you have the general outline of the events, you can begin to ask more specific questions.

There are two basic question forms: the closed, and the open-ended. Each has advantages and disadvantages.

- Closed questions are those that can be

answered with a word, or a short, precise answer. "Who was there?" "What time was it?" "Did you see a weapon?" Yes or no. Up or down. Black or white. Closed questions have the advantage of being simple and specific. However, they restrict the subject's response. And a simple yes or no rarely provides the detail of information you want.

● Open-ended questions are more general and free-floating. "What did you see?" "Who was there?" "What did you feel?" They elicit a greater amount of information than closed questions. But they require more time, they allow the subject to cover irrelevant material, and they demand more participation by the subject.

Just as there are kinds of questions you *should* ask, there are also kinds you should avoid.

● Avoid leading questions. Leading questions taint the answer by supplying information to the subject. "Jones was there, wasn't he?" "Did you see a woman wearing glasses?"

● Avoid double-barreled questions. These are actually two questions in one. "Was he drunk or doing anything unusual?" "Did you go to a doctor or mention it to anybody?"

● Avoid questions that presume information. It's easy to make assumptions about things that haven't actually been stated. "Does he prefer cocaine to heroin?" "What sorts of venereal diseases has he had?"

Maintain control of the interview.

An interview is delicate. To do it well requires a firm but subtle touch. Given the chance, some subjects will talk for hours and not answer a single question. This may be unintentional. Or it may be quite deliberate. In either event, you have to exert a certain amount of control.

Early in the interview, while you're still developing a rapport and getting a general feel for the subject, you may want to let him touch on seemingly irrelevant topics. Indeed, early in the interview, you're not always certain what *is* relevant. But don't let yourself get sidetracked. Keep your purpose firmly in mind at all times.

If possible, talk to the subject privately. The more people present during an interview, the less control you have. If the interview is at the subject's home, try to conduct it in a separate room. Or on the porch, or in your car. If the interview is in a bar, try to move to a quiet spot, away from the subject's friends.

I once had to interview some bikers in a stabbing case. I found them in the bar where the stabbing had occurred. They refused to talk to me one at a time, or even to leave the bar to sit at a table. *Faggots*, I was told, sit at a table; *men* stand at the bar. It only took a short while before I lost all control of the interview. The bikers, who had taken somewhat more drink than was good for them, began to argue among themselves about what had taken place the night of the stabbing. A fight nearly broke out and another stabbing was averted only by the bartender's threat to ban the bikers from the bar if the police had to be called again.

Controlling the interview allows you to set the pace and the tone of the interview. You can speed it up when it gets bogged down in trivialities; you can slow it down if important details are being skimmed over too lightly.

Some Subtler Points

Once you're familiar with the basic interviewing techniques, you can begin to refine them. Here are some of the subtler points to consider.

Use language familiar to the subject.

Try to speak at the same level as your subject. Not in the same style, necessarily (nothing sounds sillier than a white guy trying to talk street black), but at the same social level. Talk like a banker to a banker, like a dock worker to a dock worker. But only if you can do it naturally. People can tell if it's not natural, and they won't have any respect for you. There are exceptions, as always. If, for example, you want to intimidate the subject, start out talking at an equal social level then switch to a different level. Formal language can sometimes frighten a biker more than a tire iron, and a sudden switch to construction-worker level can show an accountant that you mean business.

Know when to use silence.

Silence during an interview almost always works to the detective's advantage. If it stems from the witness's giving thought to a matter, it certainly pays to stay quiet. Even if the silence is a product of the witness's reluctance to talk, it still pays to keep quiet. An awkward silence makes the witness uncomfortable. In his attempt to fill the silence he's likely to say something revealing. Remember, if it's awkward for you, it's agonizing to him. Wait him out.

Know when to use embarrassment.

Normally, when people see somebody embarrassed, they try to make him feel better. And when people are embarrassed, they usually try to hide it. You can use these facts to your advantage. While working on an assault case, I went to the bar where the defendant and the alleged victim, a woman, had met. I was trying to learn how they'd behaved in the bar, but the waitress who had served them was being uncooperative. While I was there, the alleged victim came in and ordered a beer. One of the patrons spoke to her and pointed to me. She walked over, threw her beer at me, then walked out. I was humiliated, but instead of trying to hide it, I let the waitress see it. She gave me a bar towel and took me back to the office. Partly as an apology and partly in an effort to explain the woman's behavior, she talked about the events of the night in question, in the process of which she answered all the questions she'd avoided earlier.

Know when to be rude.

There are times when good manners just get in the way. If, for example, the subject is blatantly lying or deliberately avoiding a question, you may want to shock him back into line. It requires a delicate touch, but an occasional demand to "cut the shit" can be effective.

Know when (and when not) to appear stupid.

It's rarely a good idea to let your subject know how much you know. Some situations require you to seem dumb as a rock. If people think you are stupid, they may let information slip out unintentionally. Or they may explain things in greater detail so that even an idiot like you can understand. On the other hand, it sometimes pays to act as if you possess all the information and just want it confirmed. If people think there is no point in hiding information, they might tell you everything.

Interviewing Mistakes

Most critical interviewing mistakes come from underestimating the subject. Not in terms of subjects as information sources, but subjects as people. Too many detectives allow themselves to feel superior to their subject. After all, *we* have the secret knowledge; *we* see the larger picture; *we* know everybody's role.

Wise up. Even the most dull-witted person can

sense emotional dishonesty. And can resent it. And can ruin your interview.

Here are some suggestions to help you avoid some of the serious mistakes of interviewing.

- *Never tell a lie that isn't true.* In an effort to establish rapport, I am sometimes less than totally honest with the person I'm interviewing. In fact, at times I lie through my teeth. I invent family members with problems similar to those of the subject; I develop ailments like the subject's; I hunt or fish for the same species; I prefer the same make of car or truck; I like or hate the same people. But, when I say these things, they're not lies. I *believe* them. I don't understand it, and it's probably an indication of a serious personality disorder, but when I say such things, they seem *true* to me. I can't tell you how to do it, but I strongly advise you never to tell a lie that isn't true. People can sense counterfeit emotion.

- *Never let your own opinions intrude.* Your convictions are irrelevant. If you are an ardent Socialist interviewing a staunch Republican, keep your views to yourself. You can debate on your own time. Do the job.

- *Never think of another question while one is being answered.* This is a common error and it can be a grievous one. Treat each question as if it is the only one you get to ask. And then pay attention to the answer.

- *Never judge.* As the poet said, we're all bozos on this bus.

Triggering Recall

People forget things. Important things, like telephone numbers and names and anniversaries and birthdays and where they put the car keys. To expect people to have a detailed recollection of an event that took place several months, or years, before requires a leap of faith that would make Aquinas himself tremble. And if that event was emotionally traumatic, the difficulty in recalling clearly is even greater.

Forgotten, however, doesn't necessarily mean gone forever. You've probably experienced the frustration of *almost* remembering something. The harder you tried to remember, the more the memory seemed to elude you. Then later, while you were relaxed and thinking of something else, that memory slipped out like water from your ear after a day spent swimming at the beach.

With proper questioning, you can induce that experience in others. A person's memory can be refreshed and a wealth of information can be obtained, information the subject thought he'd forgotten.

You *must*, however, be very careful not to plant information in the subject. While you should encourage recollection, you shouldn't prompt it. And you certainly shouldn't invent it.

There are a number of methods for jogging a person's memory. These are the ones I've found most productive. Remember, these are simply guidelines that you can, and should, modify to suit your own style and needs.

1. *Establish a specific reference point.* Find something that the subject recalls clearly and work from that. The reference point could be the time, or the persons present, or what the subject was wearing at the time of the incident. Begin with general criteria, then become more specific. Did the incident take place before or after Thanksgiving? Did it happen before or after the evening news?

2. *Cover the incident in reverse chronological order.* Most people tell stories in chronological order. First X happened, then Y, and then Z. After the subject has given his initial account of the events, ask him to tell it backward. Before Z happened, Y took place, and that was just after X.

3. *Have the subject consider the incident from a second perspective.* Naturally, people tend to report what they see from a single perspective. Anything else would lead us to question the subject's mental state. However, when asked, people can usually adopt the point of view of any person present when the incident took place. Or even a

person not present—an imaginary person. Having the subject relate the events from a new perspective can produce information the subject had forgotten.

These techniques aren't foolproof. Nothing is. But they work. And remember, they're simply guidelines for you to build on.

Body Language

I was talking to a young man who claimed to have seen my client attack a buddy of his outside a bar and stab him a couple of times with a broken beer bottle. The attack, according to the man and the alleged victim, was unprovoked. The client claimed he couldn't recall the fight—he was in an alcoholic blackout.

We were sitting on the porch at the home of the man's grandmother. He sat in a rocking chair; I was perched on a porch rail. As we talked about the participants of the fight, or about the fight itself, the man rocked quietly and slowly in his chair. But each time I asked specific questions about the events leading up to the incident, he would stop rocking.

We went through the story twice. After the second rendition, I stared at him for a moment, then shook my head and sighed audibly. I slid off the porch rail, put my hand on the back of the rocker, and in a quiet voice asked him why he was trying to run a load of bullshit by me.

It was, of course, the rocking—or the lack of it—that gave it away. The man finally admitted that his buddy had instigated the fight and had, in fact, impaled himself on the broken bottle while rushing to grapple with my client.

We're all familiar with the concept of body language. We all know that people give subtle, unconscious signals that others interpret almost subliminally. We all know it's there and we all pay some small attention to it. We just don't analyze it.

But you *can* study and analyze it. Body language isn't unique to humans. animal behaviorists spend a lot of time cataloging animal body language—the appeasement gestures of wolves, the bluffing behavior of pachyderms, the mating signals of great apes.

Human body language is subject to the same methods of study. In fact, if you read some studies on primatology, you'll see an uncanny similarity between ape body language and our own. Watch the posturing that takes place in a singles bar on a Saturday night and you'll see that people aren't much more subtle than apes. Fortunately, most people don't pick lice off each other and eat them. Not in the bars I prefer, at any rate.

Body language is, I'm afraid, too complex to cover in any detail here. Entire books have been devoted to the subject. For a complete study of the issue, I would advise you to buy one. (See the Detective's Bookshelf in the Appendix.)

There are, however, a few things to keep in mind. There are primarily two facets to body language:

- Interpretation—reading the body language of others.
- Communication—sending body-language messages.

A good detective needs to be able to do both.

Interpretation

In order to correctly decipher a person's body language, you should pay close attention to your subject's eyes, hands, feet, and general body posture. These tend to be the most expressive and reliable body messengers, and should receive most of your scrutiny.

- *Eyes:* I don't know about eyes being windows to the soul, but they're usually good for a peek into a person's emotions. A person who refuses to meet your gaze *may* be lying. On the other hand, a person who stares you down may also be lying. At the risk of sounding corny, a person who constantly shifts his eyes *may* be concealing something. I'm also told that a person's pupils tend to dilate when he's lying. Though I've never seen this reaction, it may still be true.

- *Hands:* Drumming fingers can mean anything from impatience or distraction to lying. Pay attention to see how relaxed or tense the subject's are. I've seen people smiling and laughing as if they didn't have a care in the world, and at the same time grip the arms of the chair so hard their knuckles were white.

- *Feet:* People who seem able to control all their other automatic responses often seem unaware that they are tapping or wiggling their feet and toes. Maybe it's because they're so far from the head. I can recall a man, whom I suspected to be an accomplice to a burglary, assuring me he was concealing nothing from me, while his feet were doing a frantic drum solo.

- *General body posture:* A person's posture can tell you when (or if) he is receptive to beginning an interview. Or if he is lying. Or if he's hostile or defensive or frightened or any number of things. Pay attention to contradictory messages, such as an appearance of composure while his palms are sweating. And note exaggerated postures— for example, a person who has been accused of a heinous act who appears absolutely unruffled.

These few suggestions don't even skim the surface of body language. A good detective should note a rapid increase in the subject's breathing, or a tightness of the jaw muscles, or any indication that all is not as it appears.

There are a couple of things you need to remember. First is that nothing happens in a vacuum. Each detail you note *must* be examined as part of the whole. If your subject is wiggling his foot, it could indicate that he is nervous, or distracted, or impatient. Or it could simply mean his bladder is full.

The second thing to remember is that body language only gives you limited understanding. It's useless as a method for trying to comprehend motives.

You may be able to tell that a subject is lying to you, but you still don't know *why*. Or what the truth is.

Communication

There are times when the ability to send subliminal messages is as important as being able to receive and interpret them. Take, for example, what you do with your hands. Sticking them carelessly in your pockets shows the person you're with that you trust him, that you don't feel the need to protect yourself. Jamming them into your pockets, however, can indicate that you're concealing something, such as agitation or nervousness. Hooking your thumbs in your pockets is somewhat more forward than actually sticking your hands in your pockets. Indeed, it is sometimes interpreted as sexually aggressive. What you're saying by putting your hands open on your hips is different from what you say by resting your fists on your hips.

Consider the "power stance" police officers commonly use—hands on hips, feet apart, militarily erect, the body slightly invading your personal space. It's no accident; they do it deliberately to intimidate the person they're talking to. And it works.

So be aware of your own body language. Think about what you want your body to say. Although it's usually in the detective's best interest to appear harmless, there might be occasions when you want to adopt a power stance, say, or put on a display of impudence.

Whatever message you send by body language, be certain you're doing it deliberately.

An awareness of body language should also include an awareness of interpersonal space and territoriality. Most Americans feel comfortable having an impersonal conversation with a person about three feet away. If you move closer than that, the subject unconsciously feels you have invaded his personal space. He gets a little tense, a little uncomfortable, though he doesn't always know why.

The same concept applies to territoriality. If you sit at a table with another person, you both tend to automatically divide the table between yourselves. This is my half, that's yours. If you move things onto the other person's half, again, he gets tense and uncomfortable without understanding why.

You can use these subconscious reactions to your advantage. If, for some reason, you want your subject to be distracted or uneasy during the interview, invade his personal space just slightly. A slight invasion is usually enough. Indeed, moving too close can provoke a violent reaction.

Verbal seduction works. It gets you in the door. It gets people to talk to you. It helps you control the pace and the direction of an interview. It dusts off the old memories stuck in the cobwebbed corners of the mind. It allows the interpretation and guides the sending of nonverbal messages.

It really works. If you pay attention.

Chapter 8

CIVIL WORK

When most of us think of the law, we think of the police, and dramatic courtroom scenes, and hard-eyed criminals. In fact, only a small portion of the law deals with crime. Most legal battles take place in the arena of civil law.

Civil law is the law of common crises. It deals with the problems we all encounter, with people falling in and out of love, people having accidents, people being negligent or careless, people arguing over the possession of property, people running away from each other.

A detective can help find out who did what, where, and with whom. Knowing those things can sometimes help determine who gets what when it's all over.

Much of what a detective would do, you can do. By being your own detective, you can save yourself some time, some trouble, maybe some heartbreak, and some cash.

R.G.

A wife suspects her husband of having an affair; a wrench dropped by a careless construction worker hits a man on the head as he's walking through an unmarked construction site; a sixteen-year-old girl has an argument with her parents and runs away from home; a divorced mother worries that her children aren't receiving proper care during the weekends they spend with their father.

These aren't cataclysmic events. They're the simple, common tragedies of modern life, and, in fact, the source of much of the detective's income. Civil work. It's called civil work, as opposed to criminal work. Civility, I'm afraid, has little to do with it.

Civil work may not be the stuff dreams are made of, but it *is* the stuff bills are paid by. Civil work is meat and potatoes to most detectives. It's the most commonly requested kind of detective work. It's no coincidence that civil work is also the most lucrative investigative field.

In civil work, no crimes are being committed (or at

least nobody is being charged). There aren't necessarily any villains involved. It may be that nobody is at fault. Civil work revolves around the frailties of people, people who are just trying their best to cope with tough times.

Sometimes they need a little help. They want to know if their husband is indeed having an affair; they want to sue the construction company for hospital costs; they want to find their daughter; they want to make sure their children are safe. But they don't know how.

So they call on private detectives.

Although civil work is a diverse field, most of the work belongs in one of three categories:

- Domestic
- Missing persons
- Personal injury

There is also a great deal of insurance work out there. Insurance work, however, is essentially surveillance and tailing, which are covered elsewhere.

Domestic

Things fall apart, as the poet Yeats wrote. The centre cannot hold. He wasn't talking about marriage, or whatever arrangement people use in place of marriage, but his observation is still appropriate. Things do fall apart, sometimes despite a person's best efforts to keep them together. The domestic fabric unravels.

Private detectives get involved before, during, and

after the unraveling. These are the three most common matters for domestic investigation:

- Marital infidelity
- Divorce litigation
- Child custody

They aren't pleasant matters. If they were, there
wouldn't be any need for a private detective. Nobody
calls on a detective unless he's stuck in something
potentially ugly.

Marital Infidelity

People trash around. They have affairs, one-night
stands. They shack up. Men, women, makes no difference. Infidelity is an equal-opportunity transgres-
sion.

This isn't based on any research, but men seem to
trash around more than women. That could just be a
difference in the degree of access to willing partners.
As women enter the work force in larger numbers,
there seems to be a concomitant increase in their
trashing around. Women seem to be better at it,
though, if you consider being harder to catch to be
better. Men are notoriously stupid.

Men also tend to be more consistently vindictive
when they suspect their wives or lovers of having an
affair. They want motel doors kicked in and compromising photographs taken. They want their unfaith-
ful spouses punished and humiliated. Their pride is
hurt.

Women, on the other hand, usually want information. Who is she? Why her? What does she have that

I don't have? Why is this happening? But, if a woman does become vindictive, she usually makes male animosity seem pale in comparison.

I confess, I've never kicked in a door of any sort, motel or otherwise (well, I did once; but it was to stop a suicide attempt, which doesn't really count). I *have* taken a few compromising photographs. But mostly what I've done is watch and pay attention. And I try to teach the client to do the same.

There are a number of things a person can do to determine if his or her spouse or lover is trashing around.

1. Pay attention to any marked change in sexual appetite. A sudden decrease or increase could be symptomatic. A person's sex drive might decrease from guilt, or from simple exhaustion. An increase in appetite could indicate an attempt to cover up, an overreaction in an effort to show that nothing is wrong. Or it could reflect a bolstered self-concept. An affair can make a person feel more attractive. That new awareness can boost a person's interest in sex. When you feel seductive, you behave in a seductive way.

2. Note any marked change in mood. Irritability, sudden and unusual generosity, bursts of anger or weeping. For most people, having and hiding a long-term affair is emotionally taxing. The strain usually shows in one way or another.

3. Keep track of the car's odometer readings.

Unless they travel as part of their job, people tend to drive approximately the same number of miles every day. To the office and back, for example, or to school and to the market. In contrast, people having affairs usually prefer to conduct them away from a neighborhood where they might run into people they know. The miles can add up.

4. Search the spouse's pockets or purse. Look for telephone numbers and matchbooks. Check for receipts for hotels, flowers, or gas stations in a part of town the spouse rarely visits. People having affairs are often very sentimental and will keep souvenirs of their trysts. I know a man who kept the key to the hotel room where he met his lover. Room 2102, as I recall.

5. Check all credit card receipts, instant teller slips, and canceled checks, for the obvious reason. People having affairs, and especially men, tend to buy gifts for their lovers.

6. Examine the spouse's clothing. Look for hair that obviously doesn't belong. Check for unusual smells, such as perfume or cigarette smoke.

7. Examine very carefully the reasons for your suspicion. Don't jump to conclusions. Pay attention.

8. Consider asking the lover or spouse. It's

amazing how often people will talk about their suspicions to anybody but the person who matters most.

I realize that some of the suggestions listed above are offensive. Searching the clothes of a loved one is certainly a violation of trust. So is infidelity. I only make the suggestion. The spouse has to wrestle with the moral decision.

There was a woman who suspected her husband of having an affair. Once or twice a week for a couple of months he'd been late coming home from the office. He'd claimed he'd had to work late, but on a couple of occasions she'd tried to reach him at his office only to learn he wasn't there. She didn't want to confront her husband about the matter; she just wanted to know if her suspicions were well founded.

The woman followed the suggestions listed above. She noticed that on the nights her husband "worked late," the odometer read a few more miles than normal. She'd also found a credit card receipt for flowers on the floorboard of their car.

With that information, I began tailing the man home after work. On the third day he led me to a cemetery.

Cemeteries are ideal places to check for a tail. There isn't a lot of traffic, which makes it easier to spot a tail, and bigger cemeteries have multiple entrances, so a person doesn't have to leave the same way he entered. They're also good places to meet someone you don't want to be seen with.

I couldn't follow the man into the cemetery for fear of getting made, so I parked my car and walked in. It was a large cemetery, and after half an hour I gave up, assuming he'd left by one of the other gates. I drove to the client's home and set up a surveillance on the house. The husband arrived about forty minutes later.

Twice more in the next ten days I tailed him to the cemetery. Each time I hurried to another entrance hoping to catch him. Each time I failed. I decided I would have to advise the client that we needed to hire more help to guard the other entrances to the cemetery.

As I worked on other matters during the day, I kept wondering about the husband. The cemetery routine was clever. Where did he learn it? Was he being extraordinarily cautious or had he spotted me that first night? There was nothing in his history to suggest he might know anything about losing a tail. Maybe it was a coincidence. Maybe he was just taking a short cut. Maybe.

Then it occurred to me—cemeteries have a purpose other than as a device for losing tails. They bury dead people there. A little research (and the judicious application of a fifty-dollar bill) gave me the names of everybody who'd been buried in that cemetery since the husband had started "working late."

One of the recently departed had the same name as the husband. A visit to city hall revealed the person to be the husband's father.

I spend the next three days staking out the grave. On the third day, the husband drove up near the marker and stopped. He spent the next forty-five minutes sitting in his car, smoking. Then he drove away.

I reported this to the client. Her husband hadn't mentioned that his father had died. She told me her husband rarely spoke of his father. He'd apparently been an alcoholic, a vicious drunk who had severely beaten his wife and children. The husband wasn't having an affair; he was exorcising some personal demons.

If a tail is done on a marital case, catching the adulterous couple together is only half the job. You still have to learn what you can about the lover. You can use the techniques covered in the other chapters to do this.

Divorce Litigation

The beginnings and endings of all human undertakings are untidy. At least that's what John Galsworthy said, and I've seen very little to dispute it, especially where marriage is concerned. The beginnings may be fine, but the endings of relationships can be untidy indeed.

Some marriages simply dissolve. No fuss, no bitterness, no animosity. The people seem genuinely sorry things didn't work out. Other marriages explode in flames and consume everybody involved. And sometimes innocent bystanders as well.

When a marriage explodes, people get weird. Normally pleasant people turn into creatures that would make a werewolf shy away. People who are usually kind, thoughtful, and considerate develop a sadistic streak that would make Torquemada cringe. For pure, spiteful malignancy, you can't surpass a former loved one.

I've seen couples at each other's throats over a Boston fern. Or a collection of mystery novels. During one bitterly contested divorce, I was hired to track down a dog. The couple involved in the divorce, fortunately, had no children. But they were disputing custody of the family dog. It was an expensive Japanese breed called, I believe, an Akira. They'd actually litigated the issue in court, and the husband had been granted temporary custody pending the final settlement.

A few weeks later the dog disappeared from the yard of the house the husband was renting. The man assumed his soon-to-be-ex-wife had snatched it. He wanted me to prove it (not to see if it was true, but to *prove* it) as ammunition for the divorce. He was more interested in getting his ex-wife into trouble than in the welfare of the poor dog. I agreed to look into it.

It only took a few hours to determine the ex-wife didn't have the dog at their house. That evening I followed her to her boyfriend's apartment and shifted the tail to him. I wasted the next few days tooling around after the man, watching him drive to work, shop for a new tie, and buy Chinese take-out.

But on the weekend, he and the ex-wife-to-be went to visit friends in the country. The dog was there, of course, looking healthy and happy and content.

I reported it to the client. That was my job, after all. But I refused his request to fetch the dog back. I figured the dog was better off out there. No reason the dog should suffer because its owners were acting like ghouls.

A lot of detectives refuse divorce work. Not because it isn't lucrative, but because it can get so nasty. Most divorce work consists in digging up dirt on the other spouse. This is usually done by means of tailing and surveillance, by trash examination, and by interviewing friends and neighbors. Each of these techniques is covered elsewhere in this book.

Child Custody

This is one of the most pathetic and depressing facets of detective work. In disputes over child custody one parent normally accuses the other of being unfit to care for their children. This usually involves an accusation that the other parent is neglecting, or actually harming, the children. Sometimes the accusation is a ploy in a vicious divorce proceeding. Sometimes it's just another punishment technique by the person who feels the more injured by the divorce. Sometimes it's true. There's no way to know until the facts have been critically examined.

Here are some methods for investigating child-custody matters. Remember, though, a good detective doesn't set out to *prove* anything. A detective just examines the facts.

1. *Interview neighbors.* Neighbors, if properly approached, can provide a lot of information. People develop a feel for their neighbors. They overhear arguments, they notice the hours their neighbors keep, they hear children cry. During the interview you should stress that knowing such things doesn't mean a neighbor is nosy. Information of that sort is acquired unconsciously.

2. *Interview teachers and friends of the children.* Children sometimes talk to their teachers; they almost always talk to their

friends. Teachers may also notice changes in behavior that might reflect the quality of care the children are receiving. A noticeable change in a child's grades can be a symptom of stress. When interviewing the friends of children, be certain to get permission from the friends' parents. Parents can get hostile if they discover their children have been interviewed without their knowledge or permission.

3. *Interview the children themselves.* If possible, that is. Make every effort to interview the children separately and alone. The presence of either parent could affect the child's responses. Watch for signs that the children have been coached by either parent.

4. *Photograph the children without their knowing.* A candid shot of unkempt children going to school can be very telling.

5. *Examine the trash.* Check to see what sort of food the children are being served. Make special note of grocery receipts for kinds of foods purchased. The trash can also reveal whether or not a parent is drinking too much.

6. *Be objective.* There are usually alternative explanations for any evidence you might gather. Don't read more into the situation than is actually there. It's an investigation, not an inquisition.

Child-custody matters are trying. But it is crucial that they be handled carefully and professionally.

Missing Persons

The term *missing person* is actually a misnomer; for the most part, these people aren't missing, they've run away. Wives leave husbands. Husbands desert wives. Children flee from parents, and parents abandon children. The reasons may vary, but the result is the same. Somebody who matters is gone; and somebody who is concerned wants the person found.

People who deliberately run away are usually more difficult to find than strangers who aren't where they are expected to be. But by paying attention and exercising a little patience, it can usually be done.

The difficulty in finding a runaway, regardless of age, is a factor of how carefully the person planned his or her escape. Most people don't plan very far in advance. Something happens, it's the last straw, they decide they've had enough, and they leave. If the person is an adult, they *might* prepare a few days in advance, but usually not.

The techniques for searching for runaway juveniles and adults are essentially the same as for finding strangers (see Chapter 6). The places searched, however, tend to be drastically different.

Juveniles

Kids run away for different reasons than adults do. The reasons, oddly enough, are less important with kids. What is critical in juvenile runaways is the severity of the crisis that provoked the departure. A kid might be prompted to run away after his parents refuse to let him watch *Psycho VIII*. If the kid feels the refusal is part of a long, restrictive pattern, it might be a more severe crisis than when another child runs away after being punished for wrecking the family car.

Always carry a photograph of the person you're searching for, and show it frequently. Here are some suggested steps to consider when juveniles disappear:

1. *Check with the youngster's friends.* Don't expect too much at first. Friends will usually protect each other. For a while. Eventually, the romance of it wears off and they are more likely to talk. Also be certain to talk to the parents of the friends. They may notice that Junior is spending more time than usual with another buddy, which could establish a pattern of the support network for the runaway. They may also be aware of increased spending on their child's part. Again, check the trash. Kids have a strong need to keep in touch with each other. Look for post cards, letters, notes passed in school.

2. *Check at the school.* Teachers are rarely

much help, but it's often useful to conduct a surveillance of the school beginning about forty-five minutes before classes end for the day. School, even for those who hate it, is the place to meet your friends.

3. *Check at fast-food restaurants.* Kids often hang out in such places. They can also get quick employment there.

4. *Check the youth shelters at the nearest city.* These shelters are usually sponsored by a religious group. They tend to be very cooperative as long as you aren't too demanding. Leave a photograph with them.

5. *Check bus depots.* Not just in your town, but in the nearest city. Kids are much more likely to travel by bus than any other way. Obviously, if a youngster takes a car, report it stolen. Even if the car belongs to the kid. What harm can it do?

Adults

When adults leave, they're usually more serious about it than juveniles. And they're more likely to have a plan. Even so, their plan is usually to move somewhere else and start over. Very few people go through the bother of getting false papers, assuming they know how. For the most part, they don't become different people, they just become the same person in a different place.

They usually eat at the same type restaurants, maintain the same hobbies, subscribe to the same magazines, follow the same sports. I know a detective who found a missing husband by waiting for basketball season to begin. The man, who had abandoned his wife and children in the late spring, was a passionate Celtics fan. He hadn't missed a weekend game at Boston Garden in twelve years. The detective went to the first weekend game of the season, and, sure enough, there was the man in his usual seat. He'd moved from a suburb of Boston to a small town on the coast near Cape Cod. But he hadn't been able to give up his seats. Do you know how hard it is to get decent tickets for Celtics games? The hardest part of the job, according to the detective, was scrounging a ticket to get into the arena. Celtics fans are *serious*.

As with juveniles, it's a good idea to keep a fairly recent photograph handy during the search. Here are a few suggestions.

1. *Check friends.* Especially *old* friends, like old college housemates or army buddies. Again, examine their trash for telephone calls, return addresses on envelopes, and so on.

2. *Check family members.* It's difficult for most people to totally abandon their family. There's a good chance that a runaway will stay in touch with at least one family member, although that person will probably be reluctant to talk about it. Be certain to examine family trash after birthdays and holidays (especially Mother's Day) for card envelopes with return addresses and

for telephone bills. Also interview the neighbors of the subject's parents. People like to talk about their children, even after they've grown up.

3. *Check last place of employment.* People usually give their last job as a reference for their new job. Find out if the previous employer received any such calls. If possible, get the names of companies that do similar work and companies that the subject was in regular contact with. Check them out. If the subject had a Rolodex™ at his place of employment, try to get a look at it. Business contacts are valuable; people hate to lose them.

4. *Check schools.* It's not uncommon for women, when they run away, to go back to school, even part time. In order to be accepted by any college, the subject must supply other school transcripts. Check with the registrar.

5. *Check with the subject's union.* Some occupations are limited to union members. Since people tend to take similar jobs, and since a union card often guarantees higher wages, many union members will maintain their membership. If the subject was a union member, check with his local. Although I hesitate to advise you to be dishonest, you may want to lie to them. Tell them he hadn't picked up his last check and

you need his new address in order to mail
it to him.

As in many things, timing plays an important role
in tracking down missing persons. People missing
either a very short time or a very long time are more
difficult to track down. A runaway gone a few
months is the easiest. When people have been gone
long enough to settle into their new lives, they've also
been gone long enough to start missing old friends
and family. At that point, they get careless and make
mistakes. And that makes them easier to find.

Of course, not all missing persons have run away
to start a new life. Sadly, some have run away from
life itself—they have killed themselves. Others, in a
deteriorated mental state, may just get lost and wander off. A few, mostly children, are kidnapped.

The bodies of the suicides usually turn up eventually and most of those that wander off are found by
the police. People who are suicidal tend to seek out
low spots, cellars or valleys in the woods. The lost
ones often do the opposite; they seek the high
ground, as if looking for direction. Those who are
kidnapped are rarely heard from again.

Not very pleasant, perhaps, but you knew life
wasn't all beer and skittles.

Personal Injury

An elderly woman waited at the curb for the light
to change, then began to slowly and carefully cross
the street. She'd only taken a few steps when she
heard sirens. Looking up, she saw the flashing lights

of the ambulance just before it hit her. The ambulance knocked the woman down, breaking her hip and arm.

As a result of her injuries, the woman was facing huge hospital bills. Having only a meager income, she was hoping the ambulance company would help pay the bills and hired an attorney to see if she had any hope of getting a settlement from them. I was hired by the woman's lawyer to find and interview the witnesses to the accident.

The woman didn't personally blame the ambulance company for the accident. She believed that the drivers were involved in an emergency and that she should have moved out of their way. She felt the accident was essentially her own fault. But she needed some help with the hospital bills and felt the ambulance company would be her best bet. She wasn't a crook; she was just broke. The lawyer accepted the case on a contingency basis; he would get paid only if a settlement was reached.

I interviewed a lot of witnesses, all with pretty much the same story. They had heard the sirens, they saw the flashing lights, the old woman made a gesture as if she was going to move out of the way, but didn't. Some felt the ambulance driver didn't try hard enough to avoid hitting her. Others felt the driver had made a heroic effort to avoid her. But they all agreed on one unusual fact. Although a second ambulance arrived to treat the old woman and transport her to the hospital, nobody had seen the patient in the first ambulance. No third ambulance arrived to transport the patient, and nobody saw the patient transferred from the first ambulance to the second. Perhaps the patient had expired en route and there was no longer any need to rush. At any rate, after the police had been on the scene for an hour or so, the first ambulance simply drove away.

Out of curiosity, I began to check on the patient in the ambulance. Neither the hospital nor the ambulance company would cooperate. But I learned from the police that the ambulance had been coming from a certain apartment complex. I canvassed the complex looking for the apartment that had prompted the ambulance run and eventually found it.

A heavy-set man, after eating a big meal, had had chest pains and shortness of breath. He thought he was having a heart attack and his wife called the ambulance. When it turned out to be nothing but heartburn, the man was treated at the scene and the ambulance crew left. The wife said she overheard one of the crew members say he was going to be late for a date.

And that, it turned out, was the case. We learned during a deposition of the ambulance crew that the driver had used his sirens and flashing lights to get through traffic because he was late for a date. There was no patient in the ambulance. There was no emergency. According to one of the crew, the driver was glancing at his watch when he struck the old woman.

A lot of people get injured through no fault of their own. The toaster explodes, or they slip on a newly washed floor, or they get whacked by an ambulance driver with a hot date. They did nothing wrong, yet they suffer an injury. Somebody has to be held accountable.

When such an event happens, the victim often decides to bring a suit against the folks responsible. A lawyer handles the legal issues, and a detective gathers the evidence. Here are some of the ways to go about gathering that evidence.

1. *Decide who is to be sued.* In this particular case, the decision was made to sue the company as well as the driver. The company, after all, had trained the man and the man was acting as an agent of that company at the time of the accident. Besides, the company had more money than the driver.

2. *Visit the site.* This should be done as soon as possible after the incident, because things are likely to change afterward.

   I worked on a case where a man, in a hurry and taking a short cut to visit his wife in the hospital, had walked through an area where a new wing was being added. There were no warning signs, no notice not to use the sidewalk through the area. The man had stepped in soft concrete and in the resulting fall had torn ligaments in his knee. The very next day, the area had been roped off and was littered with warning notices.

   If the incident took place in a public spot, the visit should be made at the same approximate time of day that the incident took place. That will allow you to see scene conditions most like those experienced by the victim. You may also find people whose daily routine takes them to this spot every day and who witnessed the incident.

3. *Take photographs.* Again, this should be

done as soon as possible after the incident. Photograph the scene, photograph any injuries, photograph everything. Take lots of photographs. Film is cheap.

4. *Talk to witnesses.* This is obvious. Isn't it?

5. *Get written statements.* Again, as quickly as possible after the incident. People forget things. If possible, have the witness write down his statement. But go over the information first and be sure it's in logical order. If the witness is reluctant to write down the statement, write it for him. One line at a time. And check each line with him. Get it right the first time. You may not get a second chance.

Personal injury. The operative word is *personal.* The people involved are often injured in more than a merely physical sense. The old woman who got whacked by the ambulance was made to feel frail and weak. She lost confidence in her ability to take care of herself. Even though she recovered physically, she was never emotionally the same woman.

And, in a way, that's the essence of civil investigative work. These *are* the simple, common tragedies of modern life. And while they may not be tribulations on a grand scale, they're devastating to the people involved in them. Sometimes it's difficult to remember that the measure of a tragedy is how the people involved are affected.

Chapter 9

CRIMINAL WORK

My client swore he wasn't guilty. Nothing new.

This one was a grandfather, a kindly, white-haired old man who said he had no idea why his stepson's nine-year-old daughter was saying he had touched her where he shouldn't. He loved her, he said, just as if she were his own granddaughter. He showed me her picture. She was cute, with blue eyes and blond hair in pigtails and a spray of freckles across her nose. My client told me how smart she was, how she read books, and was the smallest child in her class. He just loved her and he couldn't understand. He was humiliated because his name was in the newspaper and he was too ashamed to go to the market. And he was afraid of what was going to happen. And he cried in my office.

But he swore he was innocent and the child stuck to her story, so we went to trial.

When she testified, she had to sit on two telephone books in order to see the jury. She said Grandpa had given her milk and cookies and afterward had made her stand still while he put his hand under her dress.

She said she was scared and looked out the kitchen window. She said she watched the neighbor's kittens playing and looked at the clouds floating by and tried to think of what they were shaped like. She said she was embarrassed and didn't tell anybody what had happened. Not until a few weeks later when another girl at her school told a teacher that she'd been touched by her grandfather.

Greg and I went to my client's house after court had ended. We looked at the kitchen window. There was only the one, over the sink. All you could see was the shoe factory next door. No sky, no clouds. The neighbors had no kittens, nor did anybody else on the block.

Was she telling the truth about everything else? I don't know. My client said she wasn't. Was she trying to get the same sort of attention the other girl in her class got? I don't know.

Reasonable doubt. That's all it takes.

R.G.

Television, once again, has it all wrong. TV detectives, when they aren't skidding around corners and seducing blondes, spend their time solving crimes and catching crooks. When they help defend an accused criminal, their client is always innocent.

In real life, detectives are rarely involved in catching crooks. Operatives who work for big security firms might be in hot pursuit of pilferers, but for the most part catching crooks is done by police officers. That's what we pay them for, and they usually do a pretty good job.

In this chapter we're going to examine the private detective's role in the criminal justice system. You'll learn what really happens and why it happens that way. I'll give you a short course in criminal defense techniques. By the end of the chapter, you'll see that the criminal justice system is not a world of clarity, but a hazy, smoky world in which it isn't always easy to tell the good guys from the bad.

Private detectives doing criminal work normally

work for a defense attorney. Criminal defense work is usually considered the least attractive field of the detective business. It is typically less lucrative, the pressures are more intense, the risks are higher, the working conditions worse, and the rewards fewer. And the client is almost always guilty.

Before we examine the techniques and strategies of criminal defense work, we need to address an ethical question: If you know your client is guilty, how can you justify defending him?

You may not find the ethical answers entirely satisfactory. Get used to disappointment. So very few answers *are* entirely satisfactory.

Imagine a client, a middle-aged man, accused of sexually assaulting a twelve-year-old boy. The police also suspect him of kidnapping, raping, and possibly murdering a number of other young boys. He's already served a prison term for a similar crime.

The man is absolutely guilty of the crime he was charged with. He has admitted it to you. You believe he is guilty of the other crimes as well. All of them.

The man is a loathsome, despicable creature and a very real danger to society. Nobody in his right mind would want such a person free to roam the streets. Why should you defend him?

For the following reasons:

1. The police make mistakes.

2. Sometimes the police prevaricate.

3. Everybody is presumed innocent until proven otherwise.

4. The threat to individual civil liberties is

more compelling than the danger to individual safety.

There are, of course, other reasons. Everybody
who does criminal defense work has his own unique
set of reasons. But those are the most common ones.
Let's examine them more closely.

1. *The police make mistakes.* Not often, but it happens. We've all heard of people released after years
of imprisonment following the discovery of evidence
showing them to be innocent.

You need to understand something about police
procedures, something they don't like to advertise.
The police solve crimes in much the same way that
doctors diagnose diseases. Doctors see a set of symptoms, and, based on their knowledge and experience
with disease, they associate those symptoms with
certain specific diseases. They perform a few tests to
help them sort out which particular disease is
responsible for that illness. Then, if the tests are pos-
itive, they treat the patient for that disease.

The police see the results of a crime, and, based on
their previous experience and knowledge of the local
criminals, they associate that type of crime with certain known criminals. They perform some tests (fingerprints, witness interviews, and the like) to help
them sort out which particular criminal is responsible for that crime. Then they build a case against that
person.

Usually they're right. Usually. When the police
decide who they believe committed the crime, they
focus on that person to the exclusion of all others and
construct a case against him. It's the most efficient
way of doing it.

But what about the few times the police are wrong? They're no less convinced of the person's guilt. That's why they bring charges. They just happen to be mistaken.

We simply cannot count on the police to catch and correct their own mistakes. The framers of the Constitution realized that, which is one of the reasons they gave the prosecution the burden of proving that a person accused of a crime actually committed that crime.

2. *Sometimes the police prevaricate.* The term *prevaricate* sounds more pleasant than *lie.* Call it what you will, on occasion the police will bend the truth. They usually feel they have good reasons. Sometimes they *know* a person is guilty of a crime, they know with absolute and mathematical certainty, but they can't prove it legally. It has to be frustrating.

So they stretch the truth. Not really with the intention of deceiving the court, but with the hope of making the community safer. Their intentions are almost always good.

But we all know good intentions aren't enough. That police officers tell lies is bad in itself, but sometimes it is especially wrong. See Item 1.

I knew a man who had been arrested more than a dozen times for driving without a license. But each time the man went to court, something happened. The police or the prosecutor botched some part of the case, or a witness failed to appear, or the documents certifying the man's license had been revoked got lost in the mail. Although there wasn't the slightest doubt the man had committed those crimes, he always got off. The police were livid.

Then a police officer, one who had personally

arrested the man on four prior occasions, claimed to have seen him driving again. The officer was off duty at the time, and in his own vehicle, so he didn't give chase. But he noted the time, the make and model of car, and the location. He swore in an affidavit that he very clearly saw the man driving, and a warrant was issued for his arrest.

At the trial the officer again swore under oath that he had clearly seen the man driving a car. He was quite forceful about it, and the defense attorney could not get him to admit he may have been mistaken. Then the defense put on its witnesses. They included one of the town councilmen who testified that at the time the man was allegedly driving, he was actually in a town meeting. More than a dozen witnesses, all upstanding citizens, had seen him there.

Not only was the man acquitted, but the judge who issued the arrest warrant refused to ever again accept that police officer's sworn word. The officer eventually had to resign and find work in another town.

He wasn't a bad cop, normally. He was just frustrated at what he saw as a miscarriage of justice. So he tried to correct it. But you can't enforce one law by breaking another.

3. *Everybody is presumed innocent until proven guilty.* This is the foundation of our criminal justice system. The prosecution has most of the advantages; legions of trained police officers, detectives, laboratory technicians, and psychologists are at their disposal. All the defendant has is a lawyer and, if he is lucky, an investigator. The presumption of the innocence of the defendant and the prosecution's burden of proof are meant to help balance the scale.

If the prosecution weren't required to prove the guilt of every defendant, every single time, it would be too easy to convict the few people who actually are innocent.

4. *The threat to civil liberties.* Sir William Blackstone, the British jurist, said it was better for ten guilty persons to escape than for one innocent person to suffer. Every time a person accused of a crime is placed on trial, our legal system is on trial with him. If the law doesn't protect everybody, then nobody is safe from the danger of being wrongly convicted.

When a guilty person is set free, some part of the community is placed at risk. But when an innocent man is imprisoned, the foundation of our society is placed at risk. That's the greater danger.

What about the rights of the victim? The rights of the victim have certainly been violated. That's what brings the issue to the public forum of trial. Unfortunately, a right that's been violated can't be fully mended. It can't be retroactively protected. That applies to the victim as much as the accused. It's the responsibility of the government to mend the violation by ensuring that the guilty person be brought to trial and *legally* convicted. But the focus at the trial stage must shift to the defendant's rights; those rights can still be protected. Two wrongs don't make a right, as my mother used to tell me.

That's what justifies defending a person such as the child molester I mentioned earlier, even though there's no defending what he did. It isn't always pleasant. But it's very important.

So much for the ethics. Now for the practical question. How is it done?

There's an old defense aphorism: If the facts are

against you, bang on the law. If the law is against you, bang on the facts. If both the law and the facts are against you, bang on the table.

The attorney does the banging, but it is often the detective who provides the hammer.

Understand this. The defense team is not on a quest for The Truth. They're merely trying to protect the client's rights and to ensure that the government does its job, that it has the proof required by law to convict a person.

The techniques used in criminal defense investigation are basically the same used in other investigative work. The only difference is the direction in which those techniques are focused.

What follows is an introduction to criminal defense work. It is by no means comprehensive. It's just a quick and dirty look at the way things are done.

There are two primary methods for defending a client accused of a crime:

1. Attack the prosecution's case.

2. Build your own case.

Each tactic has its advantages and disadvantages. In some cases they can be combined effectively.

Attacking the prosecution's case.

Attacks can be made in many ways. You can—

- Demonstrate the prosecution's witnesses are confused or unreliable. Cast doubt on

their credibility or honesty. Provide witnesses who refute prosecution witnesses.

● Show that the manner in which the evidence was collected, processed, or stored
was improper.

● Offer proof that the prosecution acted illegally.

I was involved in an arson case in which the
defendant was accused of starting a fire in an apartment building. An old man died in the blaze. Our
defense was that the fire had actually been a result of
faulty wiring, that the fire had been smoldering for
several hours before the time our client was alleged
to have set it. A few days after the fire, we examined
the entire building, every apartment, floor to ceiling.
We took photographs, we walked on balconies barely
supported by their charred beams, we ruined our
clothes crawling through the rubble. We left no stone
unturned. And we found plenty of evidence to support our theory.

Then on the day of the trial, the prosecutor showed
us some photographs of the clocks in several of the
apartments. The clocks had all stopped at the same
approximate time—the time the police claimed our
client set the fire.

We were devastated. The defense had been
destroyed by those pictures. All that work for nothing.

Then we looked at our own photographs, the ones
taken just a few days after the fire. Many of the same
clocks shown in the police photographs were also vis-

ible in ours. But they were all stopped at a different time from the clocks in the police photos.

Somebody had altered the hands of the clocks. Some time after we'd inspected the building, somebody had entered the sealed building, adjusted the clocks to support the prosecution's case, then re-sealed the building as he left.

The judge, after he saw the evidence had been tampered with, dismissed the case.

Building your own case

This can also be done in several ways:

- Demonstrate that the client was elsewhere when the crime took place and therefore could not have committed the crime. In the minds of the general public the term *alibi* has become synonymous with *lie*. In fact, it simply means you were somewhere else.

- Show that the crime was, or could have been, committed by somebody other than your client.

- Show that no crime was committed.

Several years ago I worked on a bizarre case. A man had been accused of destroying a small-town police station. The town was so small that only a single police officer was on duty at night. While that officer was out on patrol, somebody deliberately drove a bulldozer into the station, backed up, and crashed into it again. The building was destroyed.

There were witnesses who saw the demolition and could identify the culprit.

On the surface it wasn't a good case. There were no apparent defense strategies. But the prosecution had to prove every element of the crime, which in this case included authorization. They had to show that the client wasn't authorized to destroy the police station.

By a fluke comment made by a witness, we learned that the property on which the police station had been built was not owned by the town. A little research confirmed the property was actually owned by a private citizen who had intended to donate the property to the town, but had failed to follow through with the paperwork. On top of that, the station had been built with donated materials.

On the day of trial the authorization matter was brought before the court. The prosecution couldn't produce the owner of the property, so there was nobody who could testify that the client wasn't authorized to destroy the building. Nobody could show that a crime had been committed.

The client walked.

To reiterate, there are two main avenues of criminal defense: attack (the prosecution's case) and build (your own case). Attack and build. Each of those avenues has two components: the law and the facts.

The law is the attorney's responsibility, so I won't devote much time to it. But a criminal defense investigator needs to be familiar with criminal law. Knowing what constitutes a legal arrest or a legal search can help you ask the right questions or recognize an important fact overlooked by the attorney. Lawyers are no less fallible than the rest of us.

The Law

In order to convict a person, the prosecution has to prove that a specific act took place, that the act violated a specific law, and that it was committed by the person accused. If it can't prove those things, the defendant walks.

What does all that mean? Consider a person charged with as simple a crime as drunk driving. The elements of this crime differ from state to state, but we'll generalize here. In order to get a conviction, the state has to prove a total of six different things. They have to prove (1) operation of a (2) motor vehicle on a (3) public way while (4) the defendant was under the (5) influence of an (6) intoxicant.

1. The vehicle has to be in operation. It sounds simple enough, doesn't it? But what if the guy was found drunk behind the wheel of a car parked along the side of the road with its motor running, the headlights on, and the radio playing? Is he operating the vehicle? What if the police find the car crashed into a fence and he's drunk behind the wheel? Can he be charged with operation? How did the car get there if he didn't operate it?

2. It has to be a motor vehicle. Again, it sounds obvious. But what if a man gets roaring drunk, rolls a car with no engine out of the garage, and coasts down the hill in it? Is it a motor vehicle? A power boat is a motor vehicle, but what about a sailboat?

3. The vehicle must be operating on a public way, a space where public traffic may operate. A private driveway is not a public way, but what if the guy is drunk enough to drive on a sidewalk? Or what if he gets popped driving on the beach?

4. It must be proven that it was the defendant who was operating the vehicle.

5. The defendant must be under the influence. Most, if not all, states have set arbitrary blood alcohol limits to determine the degree of intoxication. The standard is a blood alcohol content (BAC) of .10, although some states consider impairment begins with a .05 BAC. Reality, of course, fails to comply with the legal standard. Some folks will be able to function normally with a .20 BAC while others will be staggering drunk with a .04 BAC.

6. Finally, the defendant must be under the influence of an intoxicant. What if the guy has been taking cough medicine? Does that count?

Legally, drunk driving is a relatively simple crime. If a case of drunk driving is this convoluted, try to imagine the complexity of a homicide.

In addition to proving that a specific act broke a specific law, all the evidence collected by the police has to be legally obtained. If it wasn't, the prosecution normally isn't allowed to present it. There are exceptions, of course. In the law there are always exceptions.

Obviously, these are just the bare bones of criminal law. The more law you know, the better off you are as a detective.

I'll spend a bit more time on facts. The discovery and disclosure of facts is the detective's responsibility.

The Facts

Facts belong to no one. Facts are out there waiting for whoever asks the right person the right question in the right way. The strange thing about facts is their mutability, that is, the way they change. Ten people seeing the same event often produce ten contrasting sets of facts about the event.

The detective acts as the attorney's eyes and ears. He collects and confirms the information the attorney needs to present the defense. Despite what you see in the movies, attorneys almost never go into the field and collect evidence. There is no way they could present that evidence in court. An attorney can't call himself as a witness or personally testify against the credibility of another witness.

In concept, a defense investigator's job is simple. He merely gathers information. Whether that information helps or hurts the client is irrelevant. The defense attorney needs to know the bad facts as well as the good in order to be prepared to counter the prosecution's case.

In reality, the job is anything but simple. It is often alarmingly complex. But it can be made easier if you follow some simple guidelines.

1. *Talk to everybody involved.* The victim's version of the facts will rarely agree with that of the person accused. Does that mean that one of them is lying? Probably. But not necessarily. Each witness has a different perspective on what took place. Talk to as many of them as possible. Pay attention to what they say. Every inconsistency in their stories helps the defense.

I was involved in the defense of a man charged with knifing another guy in a bar brawl. It was a bar for bikers, one that attracted rowdy people. There had been twenty or so people in the bar when the fight broke out. I interviewed as many as I could find in the time I had.

About a third of the bikers said my client started the fight, another third said the fight was provoked by the victim. The other third refused to talk to me.

At the trial, the prosecution put on all the witnesses who claimed the fight was started by the defendant; the defense, naturally, put on the others. Of the fourteen witnesses who testified they saw the fight, none could agree on all the facts. The jury was left with the impression that none of the witnesses really knew what the hell had happened. Which was probably true.

2. *Limit your assumptions.* It would be best if you could assume nothing, but that isn't realistic. For example, it would be a mistake to assume your client is always telling you the truth. Or that the police always include all the facts in their reports.

I worked on a case where a police officer, after stopping a car, saw what he believed to be stolen property in the passenger seat of the car. The reason he stopped the car, according to his report, was because the driver was swerving as he drove. And that was true, the driver *was* swerving. What the officer failed to mention, however, was that the road was under construction and full of potholes. Everybody swerved on that section of the road.

A judge found that the police officer had no legal reason to stop the man, and all the evidence that was found as a result of the illegal stop was chucked out the window. The case was dropped.

The more assumptions you make, the fewer questions you ask, and that increases the odds that you'll miss some crucial piece of information.

3. *Examine the physical evidence.* Defense teams too often accept the prosecution's interpretation of the physical evidence—the bloody clothes, the twisted remains of the car, the detritus of crime. The prosecution's interpretation is usually correct, it's true. But not always.

For example, there was a client charged with torching a car. The only physical evidence linking this guy to the arson was a couple of candy bar wrappers. The car had been in the parking lot of a body shop, which was down the street from a convenience store.

The day after the fire, the police interviewed the people who lived and worked near the scene of the fire. The clerk at the convenience store told them she'd sold a couple of candy bars to a man shortly before the fire was noticed. The man had been a frequent customer and she knew his name. Unfortunately, she couldn't recall what type of candy bar he'd purchased. A search of the car revealed the wrappers of two candy bars on the floorboard.

The man, who was a well-known troublemaker, was questioned. When it was discovered he had a grudge against the owner of the car, he was arrested and charged with arson.

I examined the car. The seats were burned and the heat had been intense enough to melt the dashboard. The entire interior of the car was coated with the residue of thick, black, greasy smoke.

I wasn't going to bother driving to the police station to look at the candy bar wrappers. How much information could be gleaned from a pair of burned and soot-covered candy bar wrappers? But the attorney insisted and, to appease her, I went. And a good thing I did. The wrappers weren't burned. They weren't covered with greasy soot. They were just crumpled candy bar wrappers.

How could those wrappers escape the heat, which was capable of actually *melting* the dashboard? How could they avoid the greasy smoke which covered everything else in the car? How? *How?*

They couldn't. A visit with the convenience store clerk revealed that some of the firefighters had purchased sodas and chips after the fire was extinguished. And a few candy bars.

Did the wrappers found in the car come from the firefighters? Or from the defendant? I don't know. Neither did the jury.

The client walked.

4. *View the scene of the crime.* This seems obvious, but it is often overlooked. And for good reason; the scene rarely provides any helpful information. But when it does, it's usually a big boost for the defense. Juries love to look at the scene of the crime. It gets them out of the courtroom, it gives them a chance to

see how other people live, it makes them feel more involved.

I had a client who was accused of possessing drugs with the intent to distribute them. The client was known on the streets, and by the police, as a drug dealer. I'd been involved with the same client in an earlier drug case, which the prosecution lost when it was revealed the police had obtained their evidence illegally. The police were not amused. They felt it was bad enough that the judge dismissed the case; that the judge's decision was a result of their own mistakes made the matters worse. Who could blame them for being upset?

But they were more than upset. They were angry and vindictive and determined to try again. It had become personal. They wanted that person behind bars. Somehow.

And, at first glance, their second attempt looked solid. The drugs were found, according to all reports, in a locker in the cellar of the defendant's apartment.

Most of my investigation centered on the client's alibi, which was shaky at best. It wasn't until a few days before the trial that I went to the apartment where the drugs were found. The apartment had been re-rented, but I managed to talk my way in and get the new tenant to show me the cellar.

The cellar, it turned out, was shared by three other tenants. Each had a separate door leading into it. Plus there was an outside bulkhead door with a broken lock. Anybody would have entered that cellar.

There was no way to establish with certainty who put the drugs into that locker. None of the tenants, including the client, claimed the locker. The contents of the locker couldn't be traced to any of the tenants.

The jury walked through the cellar, and shortly thereafter, the client walked out of jail.

There you have it. Criminal defense investigation in a nutshell. Attack and build; law and fact. That gives us a matrix of four potential defense strategies:

1. Attack based on the facts.
2. Build based on the facts.
3. Attack based on the law.
4. Build based on the law.

That's the way it's done.

In most cases I've mentioned in this chapter, the client was released. That's not an accurate portrayal of real-life defense work. Most of the clients are guilty. Most of them get convicted. And the green grass grows all around, all around.

In many ways our justice system has little to do with justice. Our courts are *not* courts of justice; they're courts of procedure. The procedure is designed to remove the jangled and stretched emotions of the events that brought these people to court, to allow a calmer and more reasoned evaluation of those events. Although they appear to be bent to benefit the guilty, the procedures are there to protect the innocent.

It's been my experience that despite its flaws, despite its inadequacies and apparent inequities, the system works. It's slow and sometimes frustrating. But it works. And it works *because* of the procedures, not despite them.

I know a bailiff at one of the courthouses, a former police officer whose knee had been shattered in the

line of duty. He was a man who had witnessed a great
deal of pain and suffering during his career, a man
who had experienced pain and suffering himself. As
he'd grown older, he'd grown much more tolerant of
the frailties and weaknesses of others. I was talking
with him one afternoon while waiting for a jury to
finish its deliberations. It was one of those pathetic
cases in which everybody involved—the defendant,
the witness, the victim—was guilty of something,
and everybody was a victim in some way. As we discussed the people involved in the case, the bailiff told
me that although he'd become a great believer in
compassion and mercy, justice was what kept happening to people. One way or another, people tended
to get what they deserved.

Chapter 10

THE AMATEUR DETECTIVE AND THE COMMANDMENTS OF LAW

Before you set one foot on the street, before you start your car, before you do anything discussed in this book, read this chapter. This is for your own good.

Ruth Greenberg has given me a lot of good advice over the years. Most of it legal, some of it personal. But all of it was direct and to the point.

Once, when I was being badgered by a cop and on the verge of losing my temper, she touched me on the arm and said, "Don't do anything stupid." That's good advice for almost any situation. I listened to her and calmed down.

You should listen to Ruth as well. She knows what she's talking about. She's a damned fine lawyer and doesn't couch her advice in a lot of legal language. She tells you right out. She's kept me out of a lot of trouble. And she can do the same for you.

Breaking the law is stupid 99.99 percent of the time. I have, on occasion, stretched the limits of the law. I've even broken it a few times. But I've never broken a law by accident. And I've never done it lightly. The few times I've violated the letter of the law, I knew what I was doing. I weighed the risks against the potential gain, made a decision, and prepared myself to accept the consequences.

But each time, I was always right on the edge of stupidity.

Listen to Ruth. Don't do anything stupid. If she says not to do something, then don't do it.

G.F.

It would almost be easy to be your own detective if you could do anything you wanted. Torture, deep interrogation, wire tapping, and secret agents are popular and efficient investigative tools in many countries. Police detectives in these countries have an easy job.

But "a policeman's job is easy only in a police state" (*People v. Spinelli* 35 N.Y. 2nd 77, 81–2). Here in the United States, the Constitution and the law limit the police in their investigations.

You, too, must play by the rules. Here are some guidelines for what you, when you are being a detective, may and may not do under the law.

These words to the wise cannot include everything that is forbidden. Use your judgment. If you have doubts about your judgment, consult a law library or ask a lawyer. If you still have doubts, ask your mother.

1. *You're not a professional.* You're an amateur. You can do this for love; you can do it for honor; you can do it for fun. But you *can't* do it for money, or in exchange for what lawyers call "consideration" unless you have a license.

Consideration means something of value, a good or a service given to you in return for your detective work. A Porsche is goods. You may not accept ten rides in a Porsche in return for your detective work. A ride is a service. You may not accept any consideration for being a detective unless you have a detective's license. Each state has its own rules about what you need to do to be licensed, and you need to follow the rules. This is a regulated industry.

Also, accepting a consideration for services rendered takes you over the line into impersonating a professional, for which you can get into deep trouble.

Remember, you're an amateur. If in doubt, don't do anything that would disqualify you from the Olympics.

2. *You're not a cop.* In the movies, detectives carry guns and shoot people. Usually they shoot the bad guys, so nobody gets upset.

This is not the movies. Don't carry a weapon unless you have a license for it and the law of your state permits you to carry it. Check to make sure. Don't shoot anyone, even if you think he's a bad guy. And don't meddle with criminals. It's not your job. You could get hurt, or you could hurt somebody else, or you could get in the way of law enforcement people who are trying to do their job.

That's called obstructing justice, and it can be a state or federal crime. The police may not know what they are doing. You might, in fact, be able to do it better. But this will certainly not make them happy. It might even make them unhappy enough to arrest you. Even in the movies, well-meaning, smart detectives get arrested. Don't get in the way, it's against the law.

3. *You're not James Bond.* Unlike 007, you're not licensed to break the law. You may not commit crimes in the exercise of your detective work. For instance—

Don't trespass.

You can't go onto private property unless you have what lawyers call license and privilege. While it's certainly easier to look into a person's window if you stand on his lawn, unless you have permission to stand on his lawn, you're guilty of a crime. That's why it's called private property. In most states you can go to jail for trespassing. Find some other way to get the information.

Lest you get too discouraged, remember that a lot of property is jointly owned. A lot of people can grant permission to enter it. In many apartment houses you don't need permission to be in entryways, in halls, or on the roof. In others, the landlord can give permission to enter specific apartments. The tenants need never know.

But if it's private property, and you have no permission, keep off. There's very little information worth going to jail for.

Don't destroy property.

Greg mentions an incident in which he broke the taillight of a truck in order to make it easier to follow. He broke more than the taillight that night; he broke the law. Good detectives often tread a fine line. But they are paid to take risks and the good ones always weigh the costs and benefits of their actions.

You are not licensed to destroy anything, even a taillight. Depending on the value of what you destroy, you could go to jail for a while. Courts don't look kindly on those who take the law into their own hands. So don't do anything stupid.

Don't do drugs.

You may want to remain alert while conducting a lengthy surveillance. Drink coffee, eat sugar, slap yourself, but don't take drugs. There is no exception to the laws against amphetamine use, not even if you think you have a good reason. If love isn't enough to keep you going, go home.

Don't lie to the government.

Depending on the circumstances, it's a misdemeanor or a felony to give false statements to agents of the government. This includes the local police officer.

This rule encompasses lies written and unwritten, sworn and unsworn. Generally, you are not allowed give a false name for the purpose of perpetrating a fraud. You cannot deceive with the intent of obstructing justice. It is rarely a defense to such a charge that you believe in a different and better kind of justice, or higher law, or even that you were being your own detective.

On the other hand, in most circumstances, you don't have to answer any questions. Unless a police officer tells you that you must stay where you are, you're free to leave. You can refuse consent to be searched, though you might be searched regardless.

But if you decide to say something, be sure it's the truth. Or at least be sure it's not a lie.

Jurisprudence in this area is very complex. For your safety, prudence is the best jurisprudence. Remember these two simple rules: (1) you have a right to remain silent, and (2) it's wrong to tell a lie.

If you *are* questioned by a police officer, you can always ask for a lawyer. Once you ask for a lawyer, he's not supposed to question you any further. He might, but he'll probably pause a moment to consider the situation. That will give you a moment to think as well. Still, it's wiser to think first.

4. *You're not a pest.* You can't harass people. You have a right to privacy and so does every other private citizen.

Harassment is a lawyer's term of art; you can be sued for it and you can be convicted of it, but nobody can tell you exactly what it is or how close you can go to the edge without dropping off the deep end.

Professional detectives work close to the edge. That's their job. But they're bonded and insured just in case. You aren't. So I suggest you follow this very conservative legal advice. If a person says he doesn't want to talk to you, leave. If a person tells you to get off his property, leave. If a person catches you following him, leave.

If these things happen to you with any frequency, however, you should re-read this book. You're doing it wrong.

5. *You're not an advocate.* The detective's job is to *find* the facts, not to alter them to fit a desired pattern. Here are two rules to keep you within the law.

Don't tamper with witnesses.

Be careful not to get a person to change his story. It isn't that difficult to do. It can be done, for instance, by threatening to kill, injure, or shame him. Or you could offer him money or a trip to Cleveland (threat or inducement, you decide). Getting people to change their story is illegal and could earn you a long time behind bars.

You can also change people's stories accidentally. For instance, if you repeat to one witness what another witness said, you may taint the second witness's recollection beyond repair.

A good detective lets each person tell his own story.

Don't touch any evidence.

If you suspect that something is evidence of a crime, leave it alone. Don't touch it. Don't hide it. Don't move it. Leave it alone. You're in way over your head, and you could be committing a crime—obstructing justice or aiding and abetting.

You don't have a duty to turn evidence in, or report it to anyone. But disturbing the evidence may destroy material that the police, if they found it, could use. So don't touch it! Don't even touch anything near it!

Those are the only exclamation points in this book. They are here for a good reason. You shouldn't be involved with such stuff. You can't afford to play in a game with stakes this high.

6. *You're not a bus.* A bus is obliged to pick up every person who wants a ride, as long as that person has the fare. Buses are considered common carriers, and must give service to anyone who asks.

A detective is not a bus. You can pick and choose the people you work for. Just because you know how to find things out doesn't mean you have to. You're under no obligation to use your skills. Which leads us to the most important rule.

7. *You're not the Sphinx.* Many people think they have the right to remain silent. This is absolutely untrue.

If you're being questioned by a police officer or any agent of the State (except for a very few special circumstances beyond the scope and focus of this book), you do have a right to remain silent. Ask for a lawyer and see the rule about James Bond.

But if you've witnessed something, or heard something, or found out about something, a judge, in a courtroom, can compel you to tell what you know. At that point you have the right to remain silent *only* if what you say may tend to incriminate you.

For instance, if you happen to learn that a friend was hiding a stolen tractor in his garage, you are under no obligation to report that to the police. If the police come and ask you questions about the tractor, you don't have to answer them, though you still can't lie to them.

But if you're summoned to court because your friend is being tried for receiving stolen property, the judge could make you testify about what you know. Even if it breaks your heart.

Again, in front of a judge you only have the right to remain silent if what you say might incriminate you. You don't own what you know. You are the mere custodian of fact.

The only thing that keeps you from having to tell is if you don't know.

Act accordingly. Consult a lawyer if you have questions. Don't do anything stupid.

Chapter 11

THE TEN MOST
COMMON
QUESTIONS

I confess. The first time I met a private detective, I asked a lot of these questions too. We've been conditioned to think of detectives as glamorous in a seedy sort of way. We want them to be what they are in the movies, and we're disappointed to learn they don't act like their celluloid selves.

A few detectives do take on the trappings of the fictional detective. The shoulder holster, the trench coat, the hard-boiled cynicism. These guys are rarely any good. They're too busy living the fantasy.

I was at a glitzy party once where an attractive young woman asked Greg what he did for a living. He said he worked for the post office. You could almost see the woman recoil. After a few minutes of polite conversation, she wandered off to find somebody more interesting.

R.G.

When people learn you're a private detective, they tend to have one of two reactions. Either they look at you like you're an ax murderer, or they begin to ask you questions.

I've come to prefer the ax murderer response. Not because I'm ashamed of what I do, but because I can anticipate what the questions will be. They're almost always the same. They're good questions, for the most part. It's just that I'd like to answer some new ones.

It was pointed out to me that, although I've addressed some of the more esoteric issues about being a detective, I've ignored the more common ones. So here they are. The ten most common questions. Now when people ask me these questions, I can tell them to read the book.

1. *Is it dangerous?* No, not really. When you compare it with being a police officer, or operating a convenience store in a bad neighborhood, being a detective is almost safe.

On the other hand, it ain't no walk in the park. Only a fool would tell you there's no need to be cautious. It's an intrusive occupation. The entire purpose of the job is to meddle in other peoples' lives. They tend to resent that. And there are always folks who, perhaps, aren't socialized as well as the rest of us, folks who don't handle their anger very well. It can be a problem.

I once had the bad luck to irritate a group of bikers. It's a long convoluted story revolving around the sale of cocaine, a material witness to a homicide, and a house stuffed full of stolen electronic equipment. We had a little misunderstanding, which resulted in one of the biker's getting arrested. The following evening his buddies spoke with me in an alley, threatening me with something unpleasant involving a long lead pipe.

Nothing really bad happened, of course. It rarely does. I've been pushed around a bit, threatened with alarming regularity, spat on, cursed at, and generally treated like a leper. But, for the most part, people are reluctant to actually lay hands on a private detective. A fact for which I am profoundly grateful.

Given the chance, I'm a coward. People can insult me all they want, as long as they keep their hands to themselves. That old sticks-and-stones aphorism is true.

Dogs, on the other hand, were put on the earth by Satan to plague detectives. Don't misunderstand me, I like dogs. When I'm not working. But if I had to make a list of things that pose a threat to the detective life and limb, dogs would be right at the top.

Dogs would rank far ahead of drug-crazed bikers, irate husbands, and psychopathic killers. The only blood I've ever shed in the line of duty was the result of a fuss I had with a Rottweiler.

2. *Do you carry a gun?* No. Guns cause more problems than they solve. Introduce a gun into a potentially volatile situation and it escalates all out of proportion. Guns make people irrational.

As a defensive weapon, guns are vastly overrated. People have this idea (another gift of television) that all you have to do is whip out a gun and people become very cooperative. Real life isn't that neat. Show an angry man a gun and he might just decide to make you use it. Or he might try to take it away from you. And he might succeed.

Most of the ugly situations I've been in have taken place at very close quarters. Close enough to put hands on somebody. At that range, guns are as dangerous to you as they are to the person you intend to shoot (I'm assuming you know enough not to draw a weapon unless you plan to shoot somebody). You reach for a gun, the person grabs you, and you're as likely to shoot yourself as him. From a distance of five feet or more, I suppose you could draw your weapon and shoot your intended victim to your heart's content. But inside of three feet, and that's where most of the action takes place, you stand a good chance of damaging yourself.

If I'd tried to pull a gun on the bikers I mentioned earlier, they'd have followed through on their threat to do something rude with that lead pipe. Assuming I didn't shoot myself trying to get the weapon out.

Anybody who wants to shoot me will have to bring

his own gun. Besides, guns are heavy and uncomfortable to wear.

A detective's best weapon is his wits. You can talk or charm your way out of most trouble. Of course, charm is worthless on a Rottweiler. At those times a small nuclear device might do.

When confronted by those bikers, I apologized. I groveled and I whimpered. That was what they wanted. It made them feel manly and tough, and it got me out of the alley intact. We were both happy. The course of the investigation didn't change. And that's what's important.

You have to have your priorities straight.

3. *Are you ever bothered by the ethics?* Sometimes. Being a professional snoop isn't always pleasant. Manipulating people, stretching the truth, sneaking around—my momma didn't raise me to behave that way. So, of course it bothers me.

But people don't consult a private detective unless they're seriously troubled by something. They desperately want answers. The answers they get may not be the ones they want, but at least they have them. Ignorance isn't always bliss, sometimes it's torture.

Picture a fifty-year-old housewife who has never been employed and has no marketable skills. Her children have grown up and moved away. She has no family in the area. She suspects her husband is having an affair and planning to divorce her. She needs to *know*. She has to protect herself. And she can't do it alone.

This is one of the very few occupations in which moral issues aren't abstract. Concrete moral decisions have to be made on a daily basis. That's part of what makes it interesting.

4. *Is it like it is on television/in the movies/in novels?* Never. Well, almost never. I've never been *hired* to find a killer, though I have helped clear a man of a murder charge by finding the real murderer. I've never been embroiled in a case involving obscure South American poisons, but I have worked on a bow and arrow murder. I've never been asked to find a missing heiress or a kidnapped princess, but I have been asked to find a centerfold model of a famous men's magazine who disappeared with a great deal of jewelry belonging to her lover's wife. Nobody has ever tried to kill me, at least not in a work-related incident. I've never been hired to protect anybody, although I was once approached by a woman who wanted me to terrorize her husband. And I've never driven a bright red Ferrari. Never. But I'd like to.

It can't be like the movies or television or novels. Fiction has to make sense; all the loose ends have to be tied up. Real life is under no such obligation.

5. *How did you become a detective/how can I become a detective?* Believe it or not, I became a detective by answering an advertisement in the newspaper. The Public Defenders were looking for an investigator. I knew criminals; I'd been working as a counselor in a women's prison. I knew violence; I'd been a medic in the military. I got the job and got my license. The rest, as they say, is history.

How *you* can become a detective depends on where you live. Each state has its own regulations on the licensing of private detectives. In some states you have to pass a test, in others you need a minimum of two years' experience working under another detective's license, in still other states all you need to do is fill out an application and find a company to bond you. Getting bonded is often the most difficult task. Bonding companies are accustomed to all sorts of quacks coming in with visions of Sam Spade dancing in their heads.

6. *Do you use beepers and bugs and wiretaps?* Rarely. The use of high-tech snoopware is usually restricted to cases involving a lot of money. You really don't need it for most investigations.

I outfit myself mostly from good sporting goods stores. Field glasses and a spotting scope can be handy. Some of these stores also sell small-dish-antenna listening devices, which they market as an instrument for listening to birds or eavesdropping on the huddle at football games.

You can get decent two-way radios at most electronics stores. If you feel the need to buy some, get the headset models. They're less conspicuous.

A decent 35mm camera is important, as is a quality telephoto lens. Don't get too whacked out about things like infrared film or ultraviolet flashes. That level of expertise is rarely required.

There are people out there who specialize in electronic investigations. If a situation requires that sort of equipment, hire a professional.

7. *How do you get clients?* If you're good (or lucky) you develop a reputation in the legal community. Lawyers recommend you to other lawyers. Clients recommend you to other clients. Word gets around.

A few big cases help. I was lucky enough to get involved in a nasty murder early in my career.

But when most people need a private detective, they look for one the same way they look for a plumber—in the Yellow Pages. Detectives advertise just like plumbers. And often work in the same milieu.

8. *Can you make any money at it?* If you have a good reputation, yes. If you're willing to accept ugly cases, yes. If you don't mind immersing yourself in the crises of others, yes. If you have a license, yes, you can make money. Not a vulgar amount, but a decent wage.

But nobody gets in the business for the money.

9. *Why do you do it?* I do it because I like it. Because it suits me. I like being on the streets late at night, when all the good people are at home in bed. I like the people I meet and work with—the lawyers, the criminals, the cops, the desperate people.

I like the ambiguity and the uncertainty. I like not knowing exactly what's going to happen next. I like the intensity, the way everything you do *counts*. I like being able to sleep late (which is why I've done mostly criminal work, criminals keep late hours). I like the fact that every case offers the opportunity to see and learn something new. I even like the fact that, after learning something that you feel certain is important, you're not always sure what it was you learned.

I once saw a man kill a kitten. He just killed it, for no apparent reason. He was sitting in the back of a pickup truck, holding it cupped in his hands. Suddenly he just twisted its head, snapping its neck. He looked at it for a moment, then tossed the limp little body out of the truck. I knew I'd had some elemental glimpse into the human condition, maybe something to do with why some people end up as serial killers. Something horrible. I'm not sure what it was, I'm not sure what it meant. But I know that even now, years after it happened, it haunts me.

I don't like the ugliness, the suffering. I don't like the way people sometimes treat each other, the way people who once loved each other turn spiteful and bitter.

But every so often, amid all the cruelty, you see a small, exquisite act of tenderness. You see something so touching that you're never quite the same afterward. I was investigating an assault case during the holiday season and had to interview a young couple who'd witnessed the assault. They were living in a tiny, underheated apartment and were so poor they couldn't afford to buy a Christmas tree. But somebody had discarded the sawn-off end of one, a stump about six inches tall with maybe half a dozen branches leafing out of it. They'd brought this stump into their apartment and decorated it with popcorn and cranberries strung on thread. They were sort of embarrassed by the tree stump, as if I would judge them by their poverty. And at the same time, they were proud of it, and of themselves.

They were young and poor and probably borderline retarded. And they were deeply in love. Seeing the way they treated each other, the care they each took to make sure the other was happy, was like a gift.

It made redemption seem possible.

That's why I do it.

10. *Can you teach me how to do it?* I just did.

APPENDICES

Public Information Sources

The legend of abbreviations appears at the end of this section.

INFORMATION SOUGHT: Name
INFORMATION SOURCES: TD, CD, VR, CCCF, TA, CR, CCVS, UC, DMV, SOSCD
MISCELLANEOUS: A legal change in name will be recorded in the county recorder's office. Businesses often operate under a pseudonym, called DBA (doing business as); owners' names can be verified by the SOSCD.

INFORMATION SOUGHT: Address
INFORMATION SOURCES: TD, CD, PO, TC, VR, TA, CR, UC, DMV
MISCELLANEOUS: Changes of address are kept on file at the PO for at least one year. The PO charge is one dollar to do an address search.

INFORMATION SOUGHT: Date of birth
INFORMATION SOURCES: CCVS, CCML, DMV, PL(NM), NM
MISCELLANEOUS: If you have a general idea of your subject's date of birth, search the birth announcements in old newspapers.

INFORMATION SOUGHT: Description
INFORMATION SOURCES: DMV
MISCELLANEOUS: You can obtain blood type from birth certificates.

INFORMATION SOUGHT: Employment
INFORMATION SOURCES: VR, CD

MISCELLANEOUS: Rental or lease agreements usually require the renter to list place of employment.

INFORMATION SOUGHT: Marital status
INFORMATION SOURCES: CCCF, CCML, CD, CR, NM, PL(NM)
MISCELLANEOUS: Check for marriage license applications as well as for the licenses themselves. Not every license applied for is used.

INFORMATION SOUGHT: Prior addresses
INFORMATION SOURCES: TC, UC
MISCELLANEOUS: Old TDs and CDs are sometimes stored at the public library.

INFORMATION SOUGHT: Vehicle information (owner, description, VIN number, license number)
INFORMATION SOURCES: DMV
MISCELLANEOUS: Each vehicle has a unique Vehicle Identification Number (VIN), which is a code identifying the vehicle's make, model, and year of manufacture.

INFORMATION SOUGHT: Information regarding parents of subject
INFORMATION SOURCES: CCML, CCVS, CR, SD
MISCELLANEOUS: Birth certificates include such information as occupation of parents.

INFORMATION SOUGHT: Information regarding children of subject
INFORMATION SOURCES: CCCF, CCVS, SD, CD
MISCELLANEOUS: Although children are not free of the grasp of the bureaucracy, they are more loosely held. Little information is available (or important) on infants.

INFORMATION SOUGHT: Divorce information

INFORMATION SOURCES: CCCF, PL(NM)

MISCELLANEOUS: In addition to the date of dissolution, the disposal of community property, names of children, income of parent required to pay child support or alimony, places of employment, addresses, and so on are often included in the divorce decree.

INFORMATION SOUGHT: Business information

INFORMATION SOURCES: BBB, COC, SOSCD, PL, SEC, CCCF, CCCrF

MISCELLANEOUS: The SEC is a federal agency which receives reports from approximately ten thousand companies. It publishes an annual directory and will provide information about each of those companies. The PL will probably have at least one register of corporations (*Dun & Bradstreet, Standard & Poor's,* or *Moody's*) which lists subsidiary corporations. The CCCF and CCCrF will have details regarding civil suits and criminal cases involving companies. The BBB will provide information regarding the reputation of a local business.

INFORMATION SOUGHT: Information on deceased person

INFORMATION SOURCES: CR, ME, PL(NM), NM, PC

MISCELLANEOUS: Available information includes place and cause of death, survivors, disposition and value of estate, veteran status.

INFORMATION SOUGHT: Information on property

INFORMATION SOURCES: CR, PC, TA, CA, CCCF, BD

MISCELLANEOUS: These sources deal mainly with real prop-

erty, such as land and houses, and any
improvements made to such property.

INFORMATION SOUGHT: Civil legal proceedings
INFORMATION SOURCES: CCCF, NM
MISCELLANEOUS: By consulting the civil files, you can also
discover the names of lawyers represent-
ing the parties involved.

INFORMATION SOUGHT: Physician information
INFORMATION SOURCES: PL(AMD), SLB
MISCELLANEOUS: Physicians (and other professionals) are
licensed by the state in which they prac-
tice. Consult the appropriate licensing
board to learn about complaints, etc.

INFORMATION SOUGHT: Airplane and boat ownership
INFORMATION SOURCES: FAA, DMV
MISCELLANEOUS: Information on ships can be obtained
through *Lloyds Registers of Shipping and
Yachts.*

INFORMATION SOUGHT: Information on tavern owners
INFORMATION SOURCES: ABCB
MISCELLANEOUS: Includes home address, telephone
number, DBA, fingerprints, etc.

ABCB = Alcoholic Beverage Control Board
BBB = Better Business Bureau
BD = building department
CA = county auditor
CD = city directory
CCCF = county clerk, civil files
CCCrF = county clerk, criminal files
CCML = county clerk, marriage license
CCVS = county clerk, vital statistics

COC = chamber of commerce
CR = county recorder
CS = county surveyor
DMV = Department of Motor Vehicles
DOH = Department of Health
DOW = Department of Welfare
FAA = Federal Aviation Administration
HD = highway department
ME = medical examiner
NM = newspaper "morgue"
PC = probate court
PL = public library
PL(AMD) = public library (*American Medical Directory*)
PL(NM) = public library (newspaper microfilm)
PO = post office
SCO = state controller's office
SD = school department
SEC = Securities and Exchange Commission
SLB = State Licensing Board
SOSCD = Secretary of State, corporate division
TA = tax assessor
TC = telephone company
TD = telephone directory
UC = utility companies (gas, water, electricity)
VR = voter registration

Social Security Numbers

The first three digits of a person's Social Security number generally identifies the state from which the card was issued. In recent years, the large population shift to the South and Southwest has forced the Social Security Administration to allocate some numbers out of sequence.

The numbers listed below, however, are valid for the vast majority of the population. The remaining numbers identify the person. The following is a listing of the state codes.

001–003	New Hampshire
004–007	Maine
008–009	Vermont
010–034	Massachusetts
035–039	Rhode Island
040–049	Connecticut
050–134	New York
135–158	New Jersey
159–211	Pennsylvania
212–220	Maryland
221–222	Delaware
223–231	Virginia
232–236	West Virginia
237–246	North Carolina
247–251	South Carolina
252–260	Georgia
261–267	Florida
268–302	Ohio
303–317	Indiana
318–361	Illinois
362–386	Michigan
387–399	Wisconsin
400–407	Kentucky
408–415	Tennessee
416–424	Alabama
425–428 & 587	Mississippi
429–432	Arkansas
433–439	Louisiana
440–448	Oklahoma
449–467	Texas

468–477	Minnesota
478–485	Iowa
486–500	Missouri
501–502	North Dakota
503–504	South Dakota
505–508	Nebraska
509–515	Kansas
516–517	Montana
518–519	Idaho
520–524	Colorado
525 & 585	New Mexico
526–527 & 520	Arizona
528–529	Utah
530	Nevada
531–539	Washington
540–544	Oregon
545–573	California
574	Alaska
575–576	Hawaii
577–579	Washington, D.C.
580	U.S. Virgin Islands
581–582	Puerto Rico
583–584 & 586	Guam, U.S. Samoa, and other Pacific Territories

Sam Spade Conjuror's Kit

These are common tools used frequently by detectives. Every detective has individual needs and so no two kits will be exactly alike.

It's handy to have quick access to these items. I keep mine in my car, in an old medical supply bag.

1. *100-foot steel tape measure.* A 50-foot tape isn't always long enough and isn't that much smaller than a 100-foot tape. Steel is best. Plastic gets brittle in the cold and shatters if cars drive over it (don't laugh—it's happened too many times).

2. *Tape recorder.* And blank tapes.

3. *35mm camera.* Along with lenses, flash, batteries, extra film, etc.

4. *Two flashlights.* A mini-light for those occasions that demand discretion, and a huge eight-cell light for power and whacking Rottweilers. Bring extra batteries.

5. *Scotch tape.* For taping messages to doors. I've also taped a thread or a hair across the bottom of a door to see if anybody has entered since I was last there.

6. *A small tool kit.* One with screwdrivers and mini-pliers. Hemostats in different sizes are also very useful

7. *Magnifying lens.* You hardly ever need one, but it looks good, and you can use it to burn your initials on things.

8. *Other stuff.* It can't hurt to pack things like string, paper clips, breath mints, pencils, and the like. And always keep a good, sharp pocket knife.

The Detective's Bookshelf

The detective's bookshelf serves two purposes. Some of the books act as a teacher, providing you with advice on what to do and how to do it. The other books act as repositories of information, either giving you the information itself, or telling you where to find it.

What follows is a short list of books that I've found helpful.

The Way Things Work; Volumes I & II, *Simon and Schuster*

These volumes are treasures. Using simple terms, they explain many of the common technological mysteries we take for granted. The automatic door closer, for example, or clutch linkage. You'll probably never need to have a working concept of how a hay baler or a fountain pen works, but if the problem ever arises, this is the book to turn to.

The Shooter's Bible, *Stoeger Publishing Co.*

The assortment of firearms available today is mind-boggling. Stoeger Publishing puts out several illustrated books that provide specifications and related technical information for all manner of weaponry. Need to know the weight of an empty 9mm Colt Commander? Or the bullet drop of a 223 Remington Soft Point cartridge at 300 yards? It's all here.

Information U.S.A., *Matthew Lesko, Viking Press*

The federal government collects more information than anybody could possibly use. Much of that information is available to the public, providing you know whom to ask. Lesko not only tells you who to ask, he tells you how to ask for it. If you need to know the temperature at which mahogany combusts, or how many watermelons are consumed each year in Texas, this book will help you find the information.

Stedman's Medical Dictionary, *Anderson Publishing Co.*

As a former medic, I know a little more than the average person when it comes to medical terminology. But, quite frankly, I wouldn't know Nothnagel's syndrome from Renpenning's. However, I know enough to consult Stedman's.

Diagnostic and Statistical Manual of Mental Disorders, *Third Edition (DSM-III), American Psychiatric Association*

The DSM-III is not as dry as it sounds. This is the text used by psychologists and psychiatrists to diagnose their patients. It gives systematic descriptions and diagnostic criteria for all the major mental disorders and contains a glossary of terminology. It's actually interesting reading.

The Reporter's Handbook: *An Investigator's Guide to Documents and Techniques, Ullmann and Honeyman, St. Martin's Press*

A thorough guide to following the paper trail.

Crime Scene Search and Physical Evidence Handbook, *Fox and Cunningham, National Institute of Justice*

This is a basic manual on proper crime scene conduct and techniques for gathering physical evidence. It's as dull as only government writers could make it, and is obviously intended for lantern-jawed FBI wanna-be's. Still, it's a valuable guide to what police officers *should* do, but too often don't.

Miscellaneous resources:

Field guides for trees. Until I bought a field guide, one tree looked pretty much like another to me. And if I hadn't been confronted with a police report that stated the crime in question had taken place in a certain park under a stand of ash trees, I'd have remained ignorant.

A good dictionary. You don't need the massive *Oxford English Dictionary*, but you ought to have a good one. I'm very fond of *Chambers Twentieth-Century Dictionary*. It's British, which makes me feel it's more authoritative. The Brits have been speaking English longer than we have and have gotten pretty good at it.

Road guides, maps, and atlases. You need everything

from world maps to street maps. Maps do more than help you find your way around unfamiliar places. They can help flesh out sketchy information about a person and can give you the potential to ingratiate yourself. For example, if you learn that the person was born in Moss Point, Mississippi, a quick glance at the map will tell you Moss Point is a small town near the Gulf Coast. That allows you to surmise a lot of information about the person and suggests several possible topics for breaking the ice.

A guide to 35mm photography. If you need to use a camera in your work, you need to know what you're doing. You need to understand something about film speed and how it can affect depth of field and resolution. You need to know about lens focal length and speed. You need to know what to shoot and how to shoot it. There are dozens of guides to help you with the technical details of photography.

A guide to body language. If you overlook the way these guides are marketed, you can actually learn something worthwhile from them. If nothing else, they emphasize the need to look beyond spoken words.

Postscript for the Paranoid

Now you know what to look for. You know what to do. Keep your eye on the rear-view mirror at all times. Drive rental cars. Burn your trash. Lock your mailbox. Buy property under a false name. Register you car in your sister's name. Don't marry. Don't go to the doctor. Pay cash. Get curtains and keep them closed. Change your clothes often. Affect a limp. Don't visit your mother. Write nothing down. Speak to no one. Give nothing away.

Or . . . make your life an open book and live naked and unafraid.

R.G.